# THE EVEN MORE CHALLENGING

# Baseball Quiz Book

## by David Nemec

Illustrations by Herb Green

**COLLIER BOOKS**
A Division of Macmillan Publishing Co., Inc.
New York
**COLLIER MACMILLAN PUBLISHERS**
London

Also by David Nemec:

*The Absolutely Most Challenging
Baseball Quiz Book, Ever*

Macmillan Publishing Co., Inc.
866 Third Avenue, New York, N.Y. 10022
Collier Macmillan Canada, Ltd.

Library of Congress Cataloging in Publication Data
Nemec, David.
   The even more challenging baseball quiz book.
   1. Baseball—Miscellanea. I. Title.
GV867.3.N46      796.357      77-17922
ISBN 0-02-023200-4

First Printing 1978

Printed in the United States of America

# Contents

# Introduction

1978. A new season. A fresh challenge. Another World Series of baseball memorabilia awaits you.

Some of you really nailed me good last year in *The Absolutely Most Challenging Baseball Quiz Book, Ever.* I heard from a lot of you who had averages in the .400s, and one guy out in Pennsylvania claimed he went over .900 and would have done even better if I hadn't fed him so many old Federal League players. Everyone moaned about those Fed stars. Where'd I come up with all those cats nobody'd ever heard of? Surely I must have scraped absolute bottom.

Well, no. Not quite. For instance, I didn't ask you last time around who the only hurler was to win 20 games both years the Feds were in operation. You can bet you're going to get that one this trip. And there are more than a few other new wrinkles. You modern joes who lamented that there weren't enough questions about the current scene just have to turn to Game 7 and tackle the Nobody Knows My Name (1960-1977) inning.

The true experts who take whatever pitches they're given, off-speeders and zingers alike, without leafing ahead will find a sharp test in every inning of every game. Most of you managed to figure out by the end of your last battle with me that my real talent isn't so much in compiling trivia as it is in making odd connections between players no one's ever thought to connect before and in uncovering weird feats that have never been listed previously in any of the standard record books. You'll remember the old Yankee outfielder I asked you about last year who had a career average of only .025. This time you'll meet a pitcher who rapped just .016, along with the only catcher since 1894 who had a season average over .390 and the Hall of Famer who once scored 133 runs in a season and knocked in only 27! You might further be interested in discovering the name of the youngest hurler in big league history to win 20 games. And don't tell me you already know, because the answer listed in other record books is *wrong*.

Oh, I'm not infallible. I've blown a couple in my day, too. In *The Absolutely Most Challenging Baseball Quiz Book, Ever* I told you Bill Donovan was the only man since 1900 to have 25 game-win seasons in both leagues. Not quite true. If you bought it, though, you might get a kick on your own finding out who else pulled off the 25-game number. So I won't tell you the correct answer. But apologies to those of you slick enough to pick up that Mantle wasn't the only man to register 40 homers and fewer than 100 RBIs in the same season. The question should have read that he was the first man to accomplish that feat *twice*. No amends, though, for Jim Finegan; Finegan was the AL's Rookie of the Year in 1954 on just as many lists as Bob Grim.

So then, here we go again. If you hit me well in the last book, chances are you'll do even better this outing. The questions aren't any easier; if anything, they're even tougher. But you've got that extra year under your belt, and if you're smart you've been putting in a little outside homework on your own. You'll know by now who the only man was to win over 150 games and rap over 2000 hits in major league competition. You'll no doubt also know the chucker in this century who once scored 21 victories for a cellar dweller that played only 128 games! I don't doubt for a minute that you know both these things. So when you see those questions just consider them my gift to you.

Your gift to yourself will be finishing this book with a .300 average. You'll treasure every point of it too because in the pages ahead you'll once more be meeting the bizarre and the ignoble, the ignored and the unsung, the stars and the satellites—indeed, the whole cornucopia of characters who've given the game some of its greatest moments . . . and you some of yours.

Game

1

# Outstanding Offenders

*An opportunity for a fast start. Even the rawest rookie should be able to nail most of these boys.*

**1.** In 1976 Rod Carew became the first American Leaguer to post four consecutive .330-plus seasons since Ted Williams did it in the '40s. For a bingle, who was the last NL'er to rap .330 or better four years in a row?

**2.** The oldest man (by two months) in this century to win a bat title for the first time, he did it at 34. Averaging .320 over a 19-year career, he was the AL's top pinch-hitter in his finale. All 19 seasons were with the same team, and in three of them that team was good enough to get him into the Series where he stroked .321. One.

**3.** A forgotten figure already, though it's only been a little over a decade since he wrapped it up, this gardener broke in by leading the NL in stolen bases his first three seasons. Never again a leader after suffering a knee injury, he nonetheless played 12 seasons and clubbed .417 in his only Series. Since the clues are few, you get two.

**4.** Before the AL went to a 162-game schedule in 1961, he held the record for some 55 years for playing in the most games over two seasons—a grand 315 with the Reds who got into a lot of tie games in the mid-teens. Oddly, after 1916, he never again played in over 140 games. Hard two.

**5.** Never really a slugger, not once a .300 hitter, this Pirate first-sacker was nonetheless the NL's top walk-getter for several years just before World War II. As late as 1949, in his finale with the Braves, he collected 84 walks in only 413 at-bats. Two for this southy with the eagle eye who broke in with the 1934 Bees.

**6.** A shaky stick kept him from ever becoming a true star, but he was the first NL'er to sweep the stolen-base crown four seasons in a row and in 1912—his finest season—he also led in runs scored. An Ohio boy, he had the pleasure of opening his career with one of the Ohio teams and closing it with the other. Take only one.

**7.** Remembered today chiefly as a pinch-hitter, probably because he once clouted six pinch-homers in a season, this

The last lefty to hold a regular catching job.
(Question 13)

Dodger outfielder actually garnered only 19 career pinch-hits and played regularly almost exclusively during his six-year career. The first two of those seasons he hit well over .300 and amassed over 200 hits; overall he was a .308, all with the Bums. The NL double king as a rook in 1929. One.

**8.** By a margin of one home run he missed becoming not only the first NL triple crown winner in this century but also the only man ever to have a season as a league leader in hits, doubles, triples, homers, total bases and both batting and slugging averages. Tough bingle.

**9.** At 23 he won his league's MVP award, the youngest ever to do so. When he was 26 he was up for the Comeback-of-the-Year Award after suffering two dismal seasons in a row following his MVP one. One.

**10.** He had a couple of .300 seasons and was a steady performer for over a decade. Still, he never reached the stardom predicted for him as an Indian rookie in 1963. His chief claim to fame came in 1970 when he tied Dave Philley's single-season pinch-hit record while playing for the Cards. One.

**11.** Since 1892 only one man has ever collected seven consecutive hits in a game. He did it in this decade, and in his brief and otherwise totally undistinguished career he rapped only 121 other hits. One.

**12.** Your first grandslammer is on the way. Only two players in major league history who played in more than 25 games posted lifetime averages as high as .367. One of course was Ty Cobb. The second was an unsung Indian outfielder who in 1928, after an one-game trial five years earlier with the White Sox, burned up the AL for a month and was never heard from again.

**13.** Since 1894, the beginning of the modern era in batting, only one catcher who played in enough games to qualify for a bat title has posted a season average over .390. He was 31 at the time and had only one more season as a regular. Over a 17-year career, however, he smote a solid .286. Your final clue is that he's not only the only catcher to swat over .390, but he's also the last to perform a perhaps equally extraordinary feat, namely that of being the last lefty to hold down a regular catching job. Two.

**14.** This stroker never rapped 200 hits in a season; in fact, only once did he compile as many as 180. Yet he stands tenth on the all-time hit list, just ahead of Roberto Clemente. One.

*Potential Hits: 14*
*Potential Points: 21*
*Bonus Points: 3*

(*Answers on Page 163*)

# 2ND INNING
# Unlikely Heroes

**1.** Over an eight-season career he averaged only .276 as an NL gardener. In 1913, however, with the Reds and Phils, he was one of the league's top five hitters; and the following year, as a Phil, he narrowly missed the bat crown. His coda melody in the bigs was 1915, and he went out with an 0-for-7 showing in the Series. Triple.

**2.** This Oriole bonus baby was a bust for them in the mid-'50s and he was a flop once again when swapped to the White Sox in the mid-'60s. But for two years—1963 and 1964—he was one of the AL's top shortstops with the A's, rivaling Aparicio and Fregosi for All-Star honors despite limited speed and glove range. Two.

**3.** A generation ago this infielder slumped some 69 points the season following his reign as his league's bat king; the year after that he dropped off an additional 48 points, making a two-year batting average differential of 117 points. Needless to say, he never came out of that tailspin. Before his bat crown win, however, he eked out two other .300 seasons. He hit .281 over 11 seasons, most of it provided by the cushion of that one great season. One.

**4.** The Yankees had their answer to Cobb when he banged .348 in 1911 and swiped 48 bases. After a fast start in 1912, however, he broke a leg and never again approached stardom. A .214 season in 1915 as a utility man marked his finis. A generous four for this flychaser from Khedive, Pa.

**5.** His name is unlikely to come to mind in thinking of .300 hitters, but at the conclusion of the 1977 season this

AL'er had a career average of over .300 after nine seasons of play. Still, he's rated something of a flop as he's never been able to play regularly, partially because of a poor glove, partially because of an inability to hit lefties, and partially because of injuries. In 1973, his top year, he hit .329 in 100 games and clocked 12 homers. One.

**6.** The Cards wanted him bad after 1962 when he posted his second successive .300-plus season for the Cubs and pounded 22 homers. With the 1963 Cards, however, this gardener slumped to .274; and after a .230 season with the 1964 Mets, he went back to the Cubs where for the remainder of his nine-year career he played out the string in utility roles. Two.

**7.** In 1929 this Pirate outfielder pounded a .321, and the following year he led the NL in triples while stroking .313. Only 25 at the time, he looked like a coming star, but he never again broke .300. His only other season as a true regular—with the 1934 Reds—saw him rap only .258. Three for this Pennsylvania Pole.

**8.** In 1970 the Padres had an outfielder who swatted a cool .318 with 29 homers. Still around today, he's never again broken .270 or hit more than 17 homers. One for this one-year sensation.

**9.** You want a grandslammer about now? Nail this one and it's yours. Over 11 seasons this oldie third-sacker hit only .229. In 1896, however, he struck for a .328 average in his last season as a regular when the Orioles plucked him from the minors to fill in for the injured McGraw. It was his first taste of regular play since 1888 when he hit .201 for the Washington Nationals; and in 1897, with McGraw back, he was swapped to the Pirates where he reverted quickly to form, hitting only .191.

**10.** His homer in 1963 sewed up the pennant for the Dodgers. It was his first big league hit and his only one in Dodger uniform. Still around as late as 1970 with the Senators, for whom he saw most of his bigtop action, he hit only .224 in 367 games; and that one shot in 1963 is the only reason his name, mentioned today, doesn't draw a complete blank. Two.

**11.** Although considered a superstar, he's never hit over .293, has nearly as many strikeouts as he does base hits and has collected 100 RBIs only four times in an eleven-year career. Now playing in his fourth city, and the one he's supposedly wanted to play in all along, he's perhaps ready to wear the mantle he was fitted for as long ago as 1969. One.

**12.** A .280 hitter for most of his career, this second-sacker had one truly extraordinary season when he rapped .342 in 1971. Never on a division leader, much less a pennant winner, he was a sometime All-Star. After 1971, however, he slipped sharply, and 1974 found him barely hanging on with the Padres. One.

**13.** You get three if you can recall the rookie outfielder who ripped .373 for the World Champ Yankees in 1947 as a spot player and a year later, dealt to the Indians in the swap for Red Embree, hit .310 and once again played on a World Champion. The balance of his seven-year career, however, showed him to be a mediocrity, and a poor arm kept him from ever playing regularly even when his bat was hot. Swatted .262 lifetime, mostly with the A's and Indians.

*Potential Hits: 13*
*Potential Points: 28*
*Bonus Points: 3*

*(Answers on Page 163)*

3RD INNING
# The Unrewarded

*None of these former stars have merited more than a modicum of Hall of Fame attention, and some are so unremembered today that you'll be earning a fair share of extra base hits.*

**1.** Sometime in 1979 he'll probably register his 2000th hit, but no one will notice. For no one has much noticed yet that over the last 15 years, with seven different clubs, he's been one of the steadiest and swiftest bigtop outfielders. Never a league leader nor on a pennant winner, he's hit as high as .317 and has accumulated well over 350 stolen bases. One.

**2.** The AL's slugging leader with the White Sox in 1915, he slumped the next year and was bounced. The Yankees looked at him for a month in 1918 but didn't think enough of his .350 average to retain him. Finally, in 1920, he found a home in the NL and for the next eight years was one of the game's top sluggers, sandwiching the homer crown in 1924 between two .350 seasons with the Dodgers. Eighty when he died, he was forgotten by most long before then. One if you remember.

**3.** With the Dodgers and Reds for most of his long NL career, this shortstop rapped over 1100 RBIs and 2200 hits despite possessing only a .257 career average. Steady, if unspectacular, he died in 1960 at 91, unremembered although he was the first ever to play short in over 2000 games in the bigs. Two.

**4.** His name used to come readily to mind in recalling players who typified the scrappy, hard-nosed style of play in the AL's first decade, but he's not talked of much any more. Perhaps the junior circuit's best all-around shortstop in those years, he played with the Tigers, Highlanders and Nats and gave them all a rugged, fire-breathing brand of play. Two.

**5.** He played regularly for only six seasons, but in four of them he hit .300 or better and twice—with Washington in 1896–97—went over .340. He split his time about evenly between short and second, shortened his name to accommodate scorekeepers and hit .305 in over 900 games. A two-run shot for this Frenchy from St. Paul.

**6.** Between 1934 and 1949 he led the NL at various times in runs scored, walks and stolen bases. Many times he was a .300 hitter; and in 1947, at 35, he still had enough left to hit .314 for the Reds and give Reese a chase for the NL walk lead. In three World Series, his finest hours were in the garden for the Cubs and Dodgers. One.

**7.** He died in 1976, a couple of months short of his 90th birthday, hoping till the end that he would get into the Hall of Fame. It certainly wasn't an unreasonable expectation as he had better marks than many who've made it. A solid .289 average and a rep as one of the game's best third-sackers, his biggest handicap may have been that he was overshadowed for years by Home Run Baker. Still, he was on four AL pennant winners; and in 1920, at 34, he was the Indians' RBI leader. One.

**8.** Like his teammate Ken Williams, this gardener got a late start in the bigs. Twenty-seven before he first played regularly, and 29 before he really dug in, he was murder in the early '20s, three times hitting over .340, twice knocking in over 100 runs and at one time holding as many as 12 fielding records. Given his nickname you'd bingle easily; you still should, even without it.

**9.** In 1977 he played in his 20th bigtop season with his fourth team and became only the third player in major league history to play over 1000 games at two different positions. The other two are in the Hall of Fame and though this man never will be, for years he's been one of the game's smartest and sturdiest performers. One.

**10.** In 1944 he set a record by catching 155 games for the A's. Four years earlier he hit .308 as Connie's regular mask man, and as late as 1946 he still had the legs to go behind the bat more than 100 times. With five AL teams in the '30s and '40s, his fame suffered dearly because he played mainly with the lowly Mackmen. One.

**11.** From 1894 through 1908 he was one of baseball's best sluggers and base thieves. In 1898 with Washington he led the NL in slugging, three years later he hit a nifty .330 with Milwaukee, and as late as 1906 he was still quick enough to tie Flick for the AL stolen-base crown. This switch-hitting outfielder/first-sacker's misfortune was that he jumped the Dodgers after the 1899 season and thus missed a chance to get the acclaim attached to being on a pennant winner. Only in 1904, with the Highlanders, did he ever again play for a contender. Two.

**12.** Thirty-one when the NL was formed, this switch-sticker went on to play nine more seasons, mostly at second base. With the Cubs in 1878 he had his best year when he slapped .351 and just missed the bat crown. One of the best-known early day players at one time, and also one of the game's top managers for many seasons, he's dimmed badly over the years. Two for the man they called "Death to Flying Things."

**13.** He and Sam Rice are the only two men who played on all three of the Senators' pennant winners. Rice is in the Hall of Fame while this third-sacker lingers at the moment in oblivion. Not for you, though. You'll be blue for days if you don't bingle here.

**14.** Between 1928 and 1945 he caught for four NL teams and smacked .308 lifetime, including a high of .349 with the 1933 Phils. The Phils, sadly, were his main team, so he never quite got the kudos he deserved. For three years, though, he was a Gas Houser, and that clue alone should plug you in for an easy one.

**15.** Why this man has never gotten much Hall of Fame attention despite living on into his 90s and being one of the NL's most colorful performers in the first two decades of this century is something of a crime. At 36 he was still swift enough to lead the NL in runs scored with the 1913 Cubs, and 11 years earlier he led the league in triples and homers while playing for the Pirates, the chief beneficiaries of his many talents. He hit, he ran, he fielded—all like a Goliath despite his short stature—and he still holds the Series' record for most triples in fall competition. One.

*Potential Hits: 15*
*Potential Points: 22*
*Bonus Points: 1*

*(Answers on Page 163)*

---

4TH INNING
# Sartorial Splendor

---

*Just tell me the team name on the uniform worn by the performers of each of the following milestone achievements.*

**1.** Ruth's 714th homer. One.
**2.** Cobb's 4000th hit. One
**3.** Wilhelm's 1000th mound appearance. One
**4.** Cy Young's 500th win. One
**5.** Early Wynn's 300th win. One.
**6.** Old Alex's 90th shutout. One.
**7.** Smokey Burgess's 145th pinch-hit. One.
**8.** Pud Galvin's 361st win. (Hey, why's this a milestone, you ask? Because he was the first to win more than 350. Good quiz question for somebody right there.) Four.
**9.** Jimmy Foxx's 1900th RBI. Two.
**10.** Sam Crawford's first triple. Two.
**11.** Tris Speaker's 793rd double. Two.

12. Jake Beckley's 2377th game at first base. Two.
13. Luis Aparicio's 8016th assist. One.
14. Eddie Plank's 300th win. Four.

*Potential Hits: 14*
*Potential Points: 24*
*Bonus Points: 0*

*(Answers on Page 163)*

---

# 5TH INNING
# One-Year Wonders

---

*Remember the rules for this dilly? All these dudes played only one big league season—one and only one. None saw so much as a single pitch of action after his rookie season, and each in his debut played regularly at some point. Good luck, Tiger; you'll need plenty just to hit your weight.*

**1.** The Pirates planted this rangy southerner on short for the 1954 season, then dumped him after a .199 debut in 121 games when Groat returned from the service. Three.

**2.** He played 136 games for the 1911 Braves at five different positions and rapped an even .250. He looked good enough to play again somewhere in the bigs; but, alas, he never did. Four.

**3.** The Red Sox tried this 30-year-old outfielder in exactly 100 games in 1929, then slammed the door on him after a .284 lead-in. This one's in the seats with the bags full.

**4.** He played only one season—in 1959 when he hit only .218 in 152 games as the Phils' second-sacker—but you'll be mighty embarrassed if you don't bingle here.

**5.** Wanna try for another grandslam? Murmur in my ear the name of the third-sacker for the St. Louis Feds in 1914 who hit .231 in 147 games. They called him "Bo" and he lived to be 92.

**6.** Those Dodgers in the early years of our century had a lot of one-year wonders and generally weird performers. One such was their third-sacker in 1905 who hit .252 in 102 games. Some 28 years later his son got a look at the Giants' first-base job for a few days. Four.

**7.** No doubt you didn't get the last cat, and you've got even less chance to nail this next Dodger weirdie who went only .184 with a .222 slugging average as their regular third-sacker in 1904. He was good enough, though, to swipe 22 sacks, not bad considering how seldom he was on base. Three-run homer.

**8.** Another third-sacker of that era who got only one year under his belt was this heir apparent to Jimmy Collins' job with the Red Sox who was excessed after a .215 showing in 1906. Grandslam.

**9.** How about a plain old circuit clout with the sacks empty for the Oriole hurler who led the NL with 37 losses in 1892 in his only look at big league sticks?

**10.** This Phil infielder was good enough to make the rookie All-Star squad after a .221 debut in 90 games in 1945, but the Phils didn't like him enough to invite him back the following spring. Four.

**11.** The Dodgers passed this rookie first-sacker on to the Browns as a replacement for the ailing Sisler early in 1923. He hit a solid .271 in 146 games before disappearing when Sisler recovered. Four.

*Potential Hits: 11*
*Potential Points: 40*
*Bonus Points: 12*

*(Answers on Page 163)*

# 6 TH INNING
## Ole Man River

*Here they are again. The late starters, the cats who didn't really get going in the bigs until they were past 30 and some much later than that.*

**1.** As a 30-year-old rookie outfielder for the Braves in 1931 he rifled NL pitching for a deft .309. Two years later, swapped by then to the Phils, he stroked .318 and finished well up in the batting race. Moving on to the Reds in 1934, he slipped to .261 and was gone. Three.

**2.** Expansion gave this minor leaguer his first big league shot at 30 for the 1969 Expos. He quickly proved to be the most solid infielder north of the border and led the Expos in RBIs with 83. After his rookie year he dropped off some, but still this third-sacker hung on for five seasons despite his late beginning. One.

**3.** Thirty-two before he finally got a crack at a big league catching job, he responded with a .316 rookie year for the 1934 Gas Housers and a .279 follow-up campaign. Poor health plagued him, however, and he never was able to play regularly again. Two.

**4.** The Tigers gave him a look in the early '30s, but it wasn't until 1937 that he convinced the Red Sox he belonged up top. Thirty by then, he was the BoSox regular mitt man for several years before moving on to Cleveland and was still around as late as 1946. Top marks were .291 in 108 games for the 1938 Red Sox. Two.

**5.** In 1945 this 30-year-old catcher got out of the service in time to play 50 games for the Yankees. For the next two seasons he was their regular mask man before moving to the White Sox in 1948. At 35 he still had legs enough to go behind the bat 103 times for the 1950 Tigers. Big for a catcher, he had good left-handed power; and in 1946, his peak all-around year, he banged 16 homers. Tough single.

**6.** He was 31 in 1890, the year the Browns gave him his first view of the big league scene, but he didn't really stick until 1894 when Washington handed him its first-base job for the next three seasons. The Nats' top run-producer in those years, he retired after the 1897 season with a .295 average. A three-run homer for the slugger known as "Jumbo."

**7.** It's worth another three-run job to you if you name the 32-year-old rookie Cardinal second-sacker who led the NL in at-bats in 1906 while poking .262. Nothing else he did merits mention, and I won't be too critical of you if you thumb your nose at this one and move on.

**8.** Another Dodger shortstop who's worth a round-tripper is this 32-year-old who arrived in 1926 with the odd nickname of "Trolley Line." After two seasons as a Dodger regular, his trolley line switched over to the Cubs in 1928, and he was removed permanently from service after operating for the 1929 season as a Cardinal utility man.

**9.** Thirty-one before he came to the bigs for keeps, he won the NL bat crown a year later and three years after that won

Trolley Line. (Question 8)

a second when he smote .369 as a Dodger. An earlier start would have made him a shoo-in for the Hall of Fame, and you should be a shoo-in for one.

**10.** In 1952 Rogers Hornsby said this man was the only player he'd pay to see play ball. A 30-year-old Brown rookie at the time, he enticed few people to Sportsman's Park despite the Rajah's praise and was swapped to the ChiSox for whom he performed well for the next eight seasons. The AL leader in triples in 1953, he was the stolen-base king two years later. The Hornsby remark alone makes this one only.

**11.** Dropped by the A's after 1935, this backstopper bobbed up again for good eight years later at 35 with the Tigers and gave them four solid seasons. Never much of a sticker, he was an adroit handler of pitchers and had many chances after his playing days were over to offer further proof of that expertise. Just one.

**12.** He was the man Foxx replaced as the A's regular first-sacker. A 30-year-old yearling in 1925, he gave the A's two solid years of gateway duty before Foxx chased him off the post for keeps. Four.

**13.** The Giants and Dodgers got a few years of service out of this 30-year-old shortstop who first saw big league light in 1903. With the Dodgers in 1904 he slapped .265 in 151 games, his top marks. Adding that he was a switch-hitter won't keep me from offering a two-run homer.

*Potential Hits: 13*
*Potential Points: 32*
*Bonus Points: 7*

*(Answers on Page 163)*

---

# 7TH INNING
# Rookies

---

*An opportunity to score big. You won't come across any Hall of Famers, but all of these boys looked like they were headed there as rookies—and some indeed took a real run at the Cooperstown building before calling it quits.*

**1.** He once held the undisputed possession of the rookie record for homers and he still holds the Brave season mark for homers while the team was in Boston. An even .300 hitter lifetime, he was 0 for 18 in two Series' roles with the Reds, nearly matching the futility performance of Lonnie Frey, another Red of the same era. One.

**2.** He didn't win Rookie-of-the-Year honors, although he outhit the man who did by 66 points and finished only six homers and eight RBIs behind him in the slugging column. When he retired 13 years later, he had some 600 more career hits than his rookie rival, over 250 more RBIs and a higher average by five points. Yet his rival today is in the Hall of Fame and our man languishes in near oblivion. The clue that he was the NL RBI king in 1950 should tell you who we're talking about for a bingle.

**3.** A late-season trial in 1952 that saw this gardener hit .309 convinced the Reds to give him a full shot in 1953, and he showed his thanks by rapping 20 homers and driving in 100 runs. He continued his slugging through 1954, then sagged so dismally that he was down to .205 with only five homers as a part-time Phil in 1956. One.

**4.** The Cards gave this fleet outfielder a job in 1902 and were joyous when he hit an even .300 and swiped 30 bases. He dropped off quickly after that, however, and was gone by 1905. Card fans of long standing should collect a two-run homer here, but others'll have trouble.

**5.** In 1946, a big year for rookies in the NL, this Red third-sacker was right up there with the best, hitting .271 and swatting 14 homers. A year later he upped both marks, but thereafter he settled into mediocrity, although he was around as late as 1960 when he rapped .342 for the Cubs in spot roles. Take only one.

**6.** The other half of the Cubs' rookie keystone combo in 1954, he stroked .275, the same as his Hall of Fame counterpart. A solid regular for three more years, he finished as a backup to Mazeroski. One.

**7.** How about the rookie Oriole first-sacker who clouted .357 in 67 games in 1955? A dangerous pinch-hitter throughout his seven-year career, he never quite won a regular job. Finished with the 1961 Yankees after tagging 19 pinch-hits for the Indians a year earlier. Two.

**8.** The Twins seemed to have a star in the making when

this rook outfielder hit .280 and clubbed 15 homers in 1975. A year later his average slipped to .267, but he increased his homer production by five and raised his RBI output to 86. So a star he still could be. One.

**9.** The Orioles thought they had their right-field gap plugged for a long time to come when this frosh rapped 22 homers in 1964. Over the next five seasons, however, he hit only 22 more homers and just once cleared the .200 mark. No, it ain't Curt Blefary. Still should be a routine bingle, though.

**10.** Ready for a grandslam? Name the rook outfielder who came over to the Pirates from the Dodgers early in 1901 and rapped .291 in 112 games. After a .280 soph season, he moved over to the AL Highlanders, then was gone till 1907 when he resurfaced for a time with the Reds. The clue that he played the infield occasionally—one of the last lefties ever to do so—may help.

**11.** The co-holder of the AL's Rookie-of-the-Year award in 1973 after a flashy .319 debut, he's already pretty well forgotten. You'll remember him, though, for a bingle.

**12.** As a rookie he was called the Pirates' best since Traynor when he knocked in 102 runs and smacked .289 in 1936. Within a year, however, he'd given way at the hot corner to Lee Handley and never again recovered his early form. A very generous trip for those who reach back into the '30s.

**13.** Not likely you'll know the Dodger rookie outfielder who slapped .308 in 1922 and followed with a .294 soph season before being passed on to the Senators where he got in a couple weeks' work and then was pink-slipped. A lifetime .299 hitter in a very brief fling, he'll bring you a two-run shot.

**14.** The Senators liked this Alabama outfielder so well off his 1928 spring training performance that they gave him their centerfield post. He hit .302 as a rook, then vanished from the bigs after the two so-so seasons that followed. Another two-run shot.

*Potential Hits: 14*
*Potential Points: 29*
*Bonus Points: 6*

*(Answers on Page 164)*

# 8TH INNING
# Nobody Knows My Name
# (1900-1909)

*Your first glimpse at a brand-new category and one of a very few where specialists of a particular era can score big. Each game will feature forgotten stars of one of the decades since 1900, but be forewarned that the closer we get to modern times the more "nobody" will be the nobodies.*

**1.** There was a time when I used to get a flock of votes every year for the Hall of Fame. Certainly, except maybe for Jimmy Collins, I was the AL's premier third-sacker in its first decade. Jumping the Cubs to join the Indians in 1901, I was a solid .300 for several years before slipping a bit at the plate. In the field, though, I had no peer and have been called by many "the best gloveman ever" at the hot corner. After packing it in, in 1910, I returned briefly to play with the Feds. One.

**2.** A regular first-sacker for every season of the century's first decade, I played in the very first World Series and was still going strong with the Phils in 1908 when I hit .304 and stole 30 bases. My real name was William, but the gang called me by my nickname. Two.

**3.** Oh, those St. Louis teams—they just wouldn't give me what I was worth! After three successive .300 seasons, including a .339 in 1901, I hopped the Redbirds to go with the Browns. For three more underpaid seasons I patrolled their pasture, then held out until 1908 when I tried a comeback. But by then I no longer had it. Still, I was .300 lifetime. "Snags," they called me. Four.

**4.** When Snags jumped to the Browns after the 1901 season, the Birds gave me his job in centerfield and, boy, for the next five years I was tough, twice hitting .311 and finishing at .290 before the Reds gave me the gate after 1906. You got four for Snags and you'll get four more if you snag me.

**5.** I started as a catcher with the 1900 Pirates, but it was at the gateway post that I hit my stride. From 1904 through 1908 I was the White Sox regular there, and in my one

Series I was a nifty .333. Didn't have much power, true, but on the bases I could move. Two.

**6.** I was one of the guys Chesbro threw to the year he won 41. It was my rookie year, and I hung in there for seven more. You won't remember me; no one does. Even though I was pretty much of a regular for most of my days and finished up in 1911 with Connie. Two-run homer.

**7.** After a trial in 1902, I stuck the following year and starred in the first Series. I was bitter when a couple of years later the Reds dropped me after a .286 season. In 1909 the Dodgers brought me back for a look. I was only 27 then but before the year was out I was dead. I could really go get 'em out there, and as a rook I led all NL outfielders in double plays. Two.

**8.** In 1905, a couple of years out of college, I won 20, but Matty shut me out in my only Series start. Two years later, with the Reds by then, I won 17—and 11 more the following year, including two big ones near the end of the season for the Cubs. To protect my college rep I started out playing under the name of McAllister in 1902. One.

**9.** From 1904 through 1908 I was about as tough as they come on the mound for the Browns. Three times I got my ERA under 2.00, and I always won in double figures. My first big year was with the Orioles in 1899, and I also pitched for the Baltimore American League outfit along with the Dodgers and Highlanders. I had what they called a "live arm" and used to relieve a lot between starts. Three.

**10.** Before Walter came along I was the Senators' number one hose. Between 1901 and 1907 I won 104 games for the Nats and thrice worked over 300 innings. Although a lefty, I had good control; my whiffs most always topped my walks. In 1906 I missed the "charmed" 20-win circle by only one. Three.

**11.** I got in a few games in the last century but didn't really start to move until I hooked on with Connie's bunch in 1901. In 1902 I led the AL in runs scored before being bartered to the Highlanders where I tailed off a bit, though I did put in three full seasons there before departing. In my last days I played between Willie Keeler and Patsy Dougherty; not a bad pair of flankers, eh? Three.

**12.** Every inning has to have at least one killer question, and I'm it here. The Browns' third-baseman in 1903, I switched to the Nats in 1904 and stuck with them through 1905. Hitting wasn't my strong point—.216 lifetime—but in the field I was adequate. A Texan all the way, I died in Austin in 1959. Grandslam.

**13.** In 1900 I was a 29-year-old rook for the Braves. Their main arm the next four seasons, I won 27 in 1902 and then lost a league-leading 23 the following season. With the Phils in 1905 I led the NL in mound appearances and chalked up 23 wins. Control was a problem; three times I was the NL's worst in walks. Two.

**14.** For all five of my bigtop seasons I was an outfield regular. A good baserunner, I led the NL in runs scored in 1907 while playing for Mugsy. A year later, swapped to the Phils, I slumped to .215 and was released. My finest year was perhaps my rookie effort with the 1904 Cards when I hit .280 and stole 34 sacks. Three.

*Potential Hits: 14*
*Potential Points: 38*
*Bonus Points: 4*

*(Answers on Page 164)*

# 9TH INNING
# Hose

**1.** This big right-hander's lefty stick won many games for him between 1928 and 1932. At 52-37 lifetime, all for the Pirates, he led the NL in complete games in 1930 while winning 17, but fans that year were more impressed with his plate stats—a .353 average and 22 RBIs. As a hitsmith he was .306 lifetime and a heady .357 as a pinch-swinger. Oddly, he was never tried at another position when his arm started to fade. Tough trip.

**2.** The Senators acquired this well-traveled AL righty late in 1925. He won five late-season games for them despite a whopping 6.18 ERA and the following year was good for only three wins before being passed on to the Phils in 1927 for the balance of his mediocre career. Why're we talking about him? Well, because he and Johnson were the Nats' one-two mound punch in the 1925 Series, and he was the starter credited with the win in the classic third game when

Rice made his historic "phantom" catch of Earl Smith's blast into the centerfield seats. Four.

**3.** His first starting effort was a complete game win for the 1952 Red Sox. He never won another start in the majors, but in the middle '50s he took the mound 166 times over three seasons with the Reds and was the NL's top stopper of that period as he fashioned 28 relief wins and 37 saves. Cinci fans will loaf to a single; some of you others may have to hustle.

**4.** The only hurler to register more than 25 career shutouts in under 1500 innings, he was also the last chucker to win an ERA crown while working fewer than 130 innings. Sounds like he must be an oldie, doesn't it? Don't be deceived. Quite a few of you saw him. Two.

**5.** With the Cubs for the first four seasons in the '60s he showed next to nothing, but after moving over to another NL team in 1964 he was one of the senior circuit's toughest bullpen operatives for the next decade, four times registering over 20 saves. You won't need the team to rap this lefty for a bingle.

**6.** He never recorded a hit song, but in 1965 he did record the major league mark for the most innings in a season by a reliever when he was on the mound for over 165 frames with the White Sox. Marshall's since broken that mark, and Wood's since broken his AL record for most appearances in a season—also set in 1965—but you'll still single.

**7.** For a quickie bingle, who was the only chucker to ring up over 3000 career strikeouts without ever having a 300 whiff season? A bonus clue is that only once over his long career was he a league leader in K's.

**8.** The owner of the only arm to win 20 games in the Association, NL and AL made the Hall of Fame in 1946, but it's doubtful he'd have gotten there so soon if he'd had to ride in on his pitching exploits alone. Twenty-five wins with the 1895 Cubs and 24 with the White Sox six years later were his peak outputs, but he was good enough to win 242 overall. The fear that you might actually miss this one causes me to add that he was one of the game's first effective relief hurlers. One.

**9.** The accidental discoverer of the emery ball while a minor leaguer, he scored 26 wins as a rook for the 1910

Highlanders. In a short six-year career he had two other 20-victory seasons; he led the AL in losses in 1912 and the Feds in winning percentage while toiling for the Buffs in 1914. Historians will single easily.

**10.** Through before he reached his 29th birthday at the end of the 1901 season, this forgotten righty already had 167 career wins by then. Beaver Dam, Wisconsin, natives'll rack up a homer, especially when I throw in that he won 31 for the Pirates in 1895 and three years later rattled off 27 for the Reds. His first name was Emerson, but even most of the folks in Beaver Dam didn't know that.

**11.** Take a long look at this one. He was the only hurler to win games in the Union Association, the NL, the American Association and the AL, and he lived to be 94. A right-hander and a pretty fair sticker, his top show was a 23-victory season for the 1889 Baltimore Associations, but as late as 1901 he was still good for 13 wins with the Orioles. The possessor of one of the weirdest careers ever, he teamed with his brother, Brownie, for a while on the mound for the 1896 Reds. Four.

**12.** If asked who the NL's top lefty was in the early '30s, you'd of course say King Carl. But this Brave was a solid second. After leading the NL in losses as a rook in 1928, he started coming on strong in 1931 and over the next four seasons was the Braves' staff leader with 68 wins. The 1938 Pirates had him last. Good hitter. Two.

**13.** One chucker who couldn't hit a bean was this ex-Tiger and Astro reliever. On the mound he led the NL in saves in 1969 and was tough as late as 1972. His chief claim to fame, though, is his career batting average of .016. Among players who've gotten at least one career hit you won't find a worse one. Run hard for a bunt single.

**14.** His final big league appearance was a disastrous relief inning in the 1946 Series, but in the decade before that he'd had seasons in both leagues as a leader in mound appearances and relief wins. Top year was 1938 when he was 15-8 for the Pirates, but his 9-3 outing for the 1942 Red Sox wasn't bad either. Two.

*Potential Hits: 14*
*Potential Points: 28*
*Bonus Points: 0*

*(Answers on Page 164)*

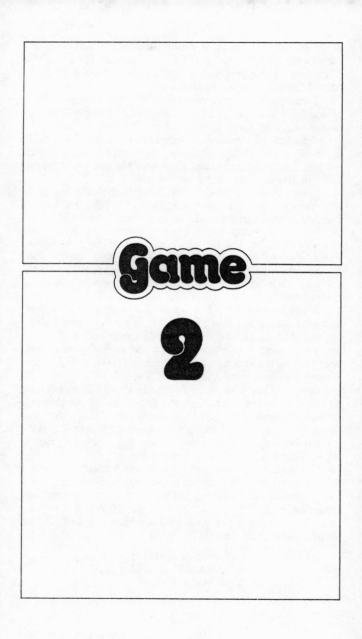

# Game

## 2

# Wine for Water

*Most often it'll be a case of a star replacing a lesser light ...*

**1.** His appearance on the scene spelled the end of Ray Jablonski as a Redbird regular. One.

**2.** Whose arrival from the Coast League made George Mc-Quinn dispensable after the 1946 season? One.

**3.** The hole left by Tony Horton's sudden and tragic departure from the game was filled by what rookie star? One.

**4.** His acquisition made Vic Saier take a seat on the Cubs' bench in 1917. Two.

**5.** The Dodgers got Jacques Fournier in 1923 just when he was reaching his pinnacle as a slugger. Grandslam for the man Jack replaced in the Bums' lineup, a man who was coming off two pretty fair seasons at age 26 but never again played a game in the bigs.

**6.** Fournier's departure to the Dodgers gave a full-time big league job for the first time to what future Hall of Famer? One.

**7.** Billy Goodman's ascendance to the bigs in 1948 caused the Red Sox to release this first-sacker, who'd been one of the AL's top sluggers in 1947. Two.

**8.** The White Stockings carried Jack Remsen's weak stick in centerfield throughout the 1878 season, then gave the job in 1879 to a rookie who quickly became one of the NL's stars and a future bat crown winner. Name that rook for three.

**9.** When he came off the campus to take over a big league job, it marked the end of George Strickland in the National League. One.

**10.** The Reds switched Heinie Groh from second base to third for the 1915 season and sent their third-sacker of the previous year on to the Phils. Oddly, the Phils put our man at Groh's old position, second base, and his work there was instrumental in their flag win. Four.

**11.** Ivy Olson was a well-traveled 31 before he found a permanent station at short for the Dodgers in 1916. Grandslam for the man he replaced at the Bums' shortstop post, with the clue that this nonentity was the wartime fill-in third-sacker for the Bums in 1918.

**12.** Rizzuto held the Yankee shortstop job through the 1954 season, then took a backseat for most of 1955 to this slick-fielding ex-Oriole. For one, who was he? Careful now, you're very likely to snap at the wrong ex-Oriole.

**13.** What former AL All-Star backstopper surrendered the Indians' catching job midway through 1946 to Jim Hegan? One.

**14.** Richie Hebner's expected debut in 1969 allowed the Pirates to put this man in the NL expansion pool. One.

*Potential Hits: 14*
*Potential Points: 27*
*Bonus Points: 6*

*(Answers on Page 164)*

---

# 2ND INNING
# Monickers

---

*Take a breath for a minute or two. But don't relax too much because if you pay attention you could get hot here. Just give me the last names that went with these wacky handles.*

**1.** Ping. One.
**2.** Little Eva. Two.
**3.** Peach Pie. Four.
**4.** Old Dog. Two-run homer.
**5.** Pig. One.
**6.** The Human Mosquito. Four.
**7.** Possum. Two.
**8.** White Wings. Two.
**9.** Old Pard. Grandslam.
**10.** Icebox. Three.
**11.** Wheezer. Four.
**12.** The Rope. One.
**13.** The Rabbi of Swat. Three.
**14.** Spook. Two.
**15.** Little All Right. Two.

*Potential Hits: 15*
*Potential Points: 39*
*Bonus Points: 4*

*(Answers on Page 164)*

The Human Mosquito. (Question 6)

# Nobody Knows My Name
# (1910-1919)

**1.** I broke in with the 1908 Reds and stayed there till 1914 when, after I started slow, they mistakenly thought I was through and sent me over to the Red Sox. For the Crimson Hose I got in two Series as their gateway guardian before calling it a day in 1918. Before another Redleg came along in the mid-teens, I held the big league record for total games played over two seasons, performing in 313 in 1910 and 1911. Two.

**2.** *Si, amigos,* for eight seasons I was one fast *hombre.* At my peak as a Reds' pastureman in 1912, I hit .317, then five years later I swiped 46 bases with the Browns. The Yankees saw me last before I said *adios* and returned to Cuba where I dropped forever from view. Two-run homer.

**3.** I started things off with the 1911 Red Sox and played through the 1922 season with Cleveland. For four years in the mid-teens I caught regularly for the Yankees, once hitting .296 in 91 games; and in 1918 I took Hank Severeid's job on an interim basis as the Browns' mask man. In 1920 I rapped a single in two Series' plate appearances. So I was far from a nobody, though a two-run shot says no one'll get me.

**4.** My first big league win was a shutout for the 1912 Giants, and my last game in 1919 came in a Braves' uniform. In between I also chucked for the Phils and Cubs, losing my only Series' start for the Phils in 1915 but coming back to win 19 for them a year later. It was me and Mayer and Alex as the Phils' big three in their glory years. Two.

**5.** In 1912 I won 23 for the Pirates and two years later, toiling for the Whales, I led the Feds with 29 wins. Too good to be blackballed when the Feds folded, I caught on with the Cubs and in 1918 led the NL in winning percentage. Finished in 1920 with 142 wins. Single.

**6.** The two other guys who played in the pasture with me my first five seasons are both in the Hall of Fame, and I wasn't far behind, compiling over 1500 hits and a .284 average. I was in three World Series and would've been in a fourth if the Yankees hadn't shipped me to the Senators for the 1921 season—my last. Humpback single.

7.  My peak years were between 1910 and 1915 when I was pretty much the A's regular catcher. Not a bad hitter, I had perhaps my best outing in 1915 when I stroked .272 in 112 games before going to the White Sox for my final season. I caught the best in my time, but it'll take the best to get me now, some 60 years later. Four.

8.  I'm remembered as a manager today, but, hey, I could play the game too! For eight years in the teens I was the Brownies' top gardener and one of the AL's best, twice leading the league in walks. After spending the 1918 campaign with Washington, I moved over to the Cards for my sunset years. Two.

9.  People forget I was not only a pinch-hitter deluxe but that I saw regular outfield duty at times too; namely with the Cubs, St. Louis Feds and Brownies. The Feds got my two best seasons—.294 and .306—but in 1910 the Reds got my only league-leading effort when I rapped ten pinch bingles. Four.

10.  I was the A's right-fielder the year they lost to the Braves. Dealt to the White Sox the following season, I had some fantastic days in utility roles and kept hitting over .300, but the Pale Hose for some reason made me ride the wood for the rest of my active days. I averaged .287 lifetime, and over .300 as a pinch-hitter. I could run, throw, do it all—and with anybody else except the powerful White Sox I would undoubtedly have played regularly. Three.

11.  For shame, Tiger fans, if you don't collect a grandslam for me. I won in double figures for the Bengals every year from 1915 through 1919 and also was tough coming out of the bullpen. Still, I'm a much neglected name, even though I lived on in the Motor City after my retirement and didn't die until I was past 80.

12.  You won't find many 20-game winners who'll bring a homer, so think hard about what I tell you. After four solid seasons with the Reds, including 18- and 19-win campaigns, I leaped to the Terrapins in 1914 and won 25. A year later, after scoring 13 for the Terrapins, I was another

one of the blackballed Feds who never again wore a big league monkeysuit.

**13.** Between 1911 and 1919 I may well have been the NL's best third-sacker. Solid with first the Dodgers and then the Braves, an injury kept me from playing in the Series in 1914. I never hit .300, but three times I was in the high .290s. At 29 I played my last big league game. Two.

**14.** At 19 in 1911 I was playing for the Red Sox. Two years later I was more or less a regular, but the problem for me always was that no one could ever decide quite which infield position was my home. So my glove did the rounds, even sometimes working in the outfield, in my ten-year career. The Red Sox were the only ones to play me steady, but the Senators, Cards and Dodgers got some good days out of me, too. In my two Series I played most at second, but short was really my favorite spot. Three.

*Potential Hits: 14*
*Potential Points: 40*
*Bonus Points: 5*

*(Answers on Page 165)*

---

# 4TH INNING
# Jack of All Trades

*Some real lulus tucked in here. Try number seven.*

**1.** For nearly a decade he threatened each year to emerge as a star, but the sad fact is he never once managed to put in a full season as a regular. One of the game's all-time top pinch-swingers, he played second, third and first and even got in a handful of games in the outfield. The Red Sox got most of his best work and gave him the third-base post in the 1967 Series when Foy slumped; it was his greatest moment—he hit .389. In over 900 games, he also played with the Tigers and Rangers, and although he's only been absent from the scene for five years, take a gift double for him.

**2.** Starting with the Cubs in 1922, he played regularly at three different infield positions for four clubs over the next

13 seasons. Three years in a row he led the NL in at-bats, and in 1931, with the Cards, he led in doubles. His best work was at second, but he also played short, third and occasionally the outfield. Solid all the way despite being only 5' 5½". Very tough single.

**3.** A two-run homer in your column for this oldie first-sacker who also played regularly behind the bat and in the outfield. Top year was a .329 showing for the 1897 Cards before he moved over to the Phils where he played the next seven seasons. Since his nickname would give it to you, you'll have to score without it.

**4.** Known today for assembling the powerful Oriole International League dynasty in the century's early years, he was actually a fine player in his own right. He played the outfield, all the infield positions except first base and was good enough on the mound to win 23 for the 1899 Dodgers. Should be a snap bingle.

**5.** Between 1919 and 1933 he played every big league position. Third and second were his most common roosting places, although he hit .301 for the Phils as their shortstop in 1929. Six years earlier, at third for the Cubs, he had his finest all-around year, hitting .318 and clubbing 12 homers; but I can't argue much with those who vote for 1930 when, in utility roles, he hit .341 for the Phils in 105 games. Take three for this jack whom time's forgotten.

**6.** Through the 1940s this six-footer played regularly for the Pirates at second, third and short. A first-stringer at age 20, he started to slip badly at 28 and was passed on to the Cubs. After a year in Chi as a backup to Serena, he was waived to the Browns and played his last game at 30. Still, he accumulated over 1200 hits, and in 1947—his top year— he hit .297 and scored 102 runs. Just one.

**7.** A grandslam alert! You'll savor it if you get this next mystery man from the AL's early years. After three games with the 1900 Cubs, he moved to the White Sox in 1901 and was switched to the Indians at midseason. Through in 1902 at 24 after only 76 big league games, he was a mere 3-6 as a moundsman; but as a part-time outfielder he rapped .332 and stole an amazing 17 bases. You won't get 'em much tougher than the kid they called "Zaza."

**8.** Between 1898 and 1909 he played every position on the diamond. A rookie with the 1898 Cubs, he dropped off the big league map until 1901 when the White Sox gave him their first-base job. Later they moved him to second, his station in his only Series in 1906. A .252 batsman, he was also 4-7 as an occasional chucker. The AL's stolen base champ in its maiden season. Two.

**9.** He divided his career about equally between the outfield and the mound, making the transition to the rubber in 1954 after six seasons as a strong-armed but weak-sticked Cub outfielder. As an indication of how little clout he had, not once while a pitcher—in six seasons, no less!—was he called on to pinch-hit. Primarily a reliever as a moundsman, his top year was 12-13 for the 1957 Reds who used him mostly as a starter that season. His stick did its best job in 1948 when he hit .279 as a rookie Bruin centerfielder. One.

**10.** Baseball's early years were filled with great all-around players, but few were more versatile than this old Boston star who played every position in a 15-year career. Usually a first-sacker, he could as easily be found at any of the other three infield positions, and for eight seasons in the 1880s he was a player/manager. Two for this early day jack who was known as "Honest John."

**11.** As a rookie with the 1909 Pirates he saw regular duty at second base; but by 1912 he was at first, and in his 1921 finale with the Phils he played mostly at third. In the years between, most of them with the Cards, he also played a fair amount of short. Three for another jack named John, with the hint that he played under a rather odd nickname.

*Potential Hits: 11*
*Potential Points: 24*
*Bonus Points: 4*

*(Answers on Page 165)*

---

$5$TH INNING
# Team Teasers

---

**1.** The Tigers in the 1920s split their catching job for most of the decade between two men. Both had good eyes and were .300 hitters at times, and one in fact retired after the

1927 season with a .304 average. But power hitters they were not. Between them they batted over 3600 times in the majors, and each knocked only one homer. This bit of eso-terica is worth a two-run shot if you can name both of these powerless mask men. Just a single, though, for one.

**2.** Chick Fraser had many distinctions. His most interest-ing, though, was that his only two 20-victory seasons came around the turn of the century for two different teams in two different leagues who played out of the same city. The odds on this are so short that you almost can't miss collect-ing one for the city.

**3.** Only once in major league history has a team had three 40-homer men in the same season. Name the team, the three sluggers and the year and you get two. It's not all that hard, kiddo.

**4.** In 1943 this wartime AL team finished fifth despite hav-ing a big four who among them totaled 748 career victories. The team's worth one, and the four men will bring an additional three. Zip for the men unless you get all four.

**5.** What was the first team to field better than .950 in a season? Homer for the club; grandslam if you can come within one of the year.

**6.** In 1904 each league had a team that played a full 154-game schedule. They were the first two clubs to do that number. A homer if you nail both in two guesses; single for only one right.

**7.** Quick now, what pennant winner had the lowest season winning percentage? Simple one.

**8.** After falling into the NL cellar in 1947, the Pirates bounced back in 1948 to finish a sturdy fourth. One of the main reasons for their sharp reversal was the play of their infield that year. All four regulars came through with solid seasons, and each was still young enough to give Pirate fans pennant hopes for 1949. What happened, though, was one of the saddest chapters in Corsair history. Their first-sacker in 1948 played only part-time thereafter and was gone in 1950 at age 25; the man at second slumped from .290 to .203 and lost the job to the not-exactly-immortal Montie Basgall; the third-sacker was swapped to the Cubs and never played regularly again; and the shortstop, who had led the NL in at-bats and assists in 1948, fell off from .290 to .244 and was demoted to utility roles after 1949.

Four if you can name this luckless quartet, two if you know only three and zip for less.

**9.** Only one club in history has had four 20-game losers in a single season. Moreover, it happened two years in a row. Telling you this disaster occurred in the early 1900s will be your only clue. Now tell me the team for a bingle. Three more bases if you can name six of the seven hurlers who were part of the unhappy number.

**10.** Mike Tresh slipped badly after the 1947 season, and it was to be another four years before the White Sox would deal for Lollar. What happened to the Pale Hose catching corps over those four seasons between 1948 and 1951 is unreal. Including Tresh, no fewer than 14 men wore the Pale Hose tools of the trade in that interval. Four if you can name ten or more in 14 guesses. Two for eight right. A goose egg for less.

**11.** The 1938 Cubs got important contributions from three former Gas Housers on their way to the NL flag. Get all three and I'll cough up one.

**12.** In 1887 the Wolverines copped the NL flag while winning only 79 games. Only one pennant winner in the years since has won fewer than 80 games. With the clue that it happened after 1900, the year should flash in quickly. So will the team, with a little more thought. One.

**13.** The 1944 Browns were a motley collection of retreads and fuzzy cheeks. Their only .300 hitter, however, was a bona fide big league regular for many years. For a deuce, who was he?

**14.** The old Senators went from Washington to Minnesota in 1961. The new Senators fled for Texas in 1972. One sticker played on both versions of the Senators as well as the Twins and Rangers. After being told that he also played for the A's, Angels, and Pilots, you can't miss a bingle.

*Potential Hits: 14*
*Potential Points: 37*
*Bonus Points: 4*

*(Answers on Page 165)*

# It's All Relative

**1.** The only trio of brothers to compile over 1000 big league hits each was not the DiMaggios. For one, who were they?

**2.** From 1969 through 1974 these two brothers played for rival AL teams. The elder, a shortstop, was perennially handicapped by a weak mace. His brother, a catcher, was even worse at the plate, rapping only .172 in 148 games. One for these Cinci sibs.

**3.** In 1898 these two brothers played a few games beside each other in the Louisville pasture, but one had to wait another ten seasons before he had his sole chance to play regularly. Oddly, both brothers in 1908 missed becoming, by only a game and a half, the first sibs to play against each other in a World Series, as the younger boy's club finished just half a game off the pace and the elder's outfit, which he also happened to manage, trailed the Cubs by a scant game. For four name them both; no credit for just telling me the Hall of Fame elder.

**4.** In 1927 a rookie Senator outfielder hit .438 in 13 games. Twenty years earlier his uncle led the NL in triples, playing first base for the Reds, and 20 years before that the lad's father caught for the pennant-winning Wolverines. Use these sketchy clues to nail the last name of this famous baseball family and you'll earn two.

**5.** In 1944 this rookie won the regular Yankee catching job; his older brother meanwhile was Frankie Hayes' backup man. The following season both caught again in the AL—Mike, the younger, with the Yankees, and Bob, the elder, with the Red Sox. Bob had several seasons in the '30s as a bullpen operative. For three, give me the last name of these backstopping brothers.

**6.** The A's just missed having a brother battery when they gave the catching half his walking papers after the 1968 season and then brought up the mound half in 1969 to fill out their bullpen corps. Neither exactly set heads spinning with his big league efforts, though the catcher was a regular for a time in 1965 and the hurler got in 41 games in 1970. Bet two you don't remember them.

**7.** These two sibs played side by side in the infield for the 1882 Browns—Bill, the younger, at short, and Jack at third. Both enjoyed several bigtop seasons, and Bill was a member of the Brownie powerhouse teams later in the decade. But 1882 was their only full year as teammates. For a homer, do you know them?

**8.** These two brothers were born 24 years apart. Ham, the elder, got in a scattering of games for the 1909 Browns and showed nothing. But Pat banged .400 for the 1921 Giants in 23 games before an injury ended his very promising infield career. Two-run shot for the last name.

**9.** This promising Indian infielder had his career nearly ruined in 1940 when a batting practice liner slammed him in the face. Some 20 years earlier, his father, a star Cub first-sacker, also had injuries curtail his career after a .354 season. Single for this ill-fated father-and-son duo, and a free clue that the father's brother played in the bigs with the Giants for a time.

**10.** Both these brothers finished their long careers in 1945, the elder in the Series with the Tigers and the younger with the Reds. Oddly, they played side by side as rookie outfielders for the 1931 Tigers, and the younger also saw Series action with the Bengals while the older played a couple of seasons with the Reds. The parallels abound for these two brothers, and after telling you that the younger sib came only nine hits short of banging 2000, I'm giving only one.

**11.** Charlie got in only a handful of games with the A's in 1919 and 1920, but his two older brothers were both bigtop regulars, the elder an outfielder in the teens with the Yankees and the middle and most famous sib a third-sacker with the Dodgers, Braves and Cardinals. Seeing action in three Series with the Cards, the middle brother gave way finally as a regular to Pepper Martin. One for the last name.

**12.** These two brothers presently hold the record for the most World Series hits and total bases by two siblings, each of whom played in more than one Series. That of course eliminates the DiMaggios, but there's no trick here since in their time this pair was as well known as the DiMaggios. Both won RBI crowns, both had many .300 seasons, and together they had the added distinction of being the second pair of sibs ever to play against each other in a World Series. One.

*Potential Hits: 12*
*Potential Points: 25*
*Bonus Points: 1*

(*Answers on Page 165*)

---

# 7TH INNING
## Teen Terrors

---

*You'll get three looks at this one, so rise to it and enjoy yourself. All these babes in the dugout saw big league action before they were 20, and more than one had already gone back to mom on the farm before he was old enough to vote.*

**1.** Starting off with a fat one: Name the 18-year-old Athletic righty who scored a quick shutout in 1961 but had to wait five years to ring up his second. Solid with the A's in the late '60s, he led off the '70s as one of the Brewers' main arms.

**2.** How about the 19-year-old who won 34 for the Browns in 1887 and 45 a year later? Through before he was 30, he still rang up over 200 career wins. Two.

**3.** He played his first game with the White Sox when he was 17 and was their wartime shortstop in 1945 at a ripe 19. By the time he was 27 he had over 1000 hits, but a near fatal injury stopped him a year later. Single.

**4.** This next White Soxer'll bring a grandslam. At 18 in 1949 he hit .400 in eight games while showcasing his youthful wares at shortstop. Twelve years went by in the minors before he surfaced again, albeit briefly, hitting .125 for the NL champ Reds as an occasional relief man for Blasingame.

**5.** The Cubs looked at this 19-year-old gardener for the first time in 1960. They took their last peek at him in 1963, then sent him over to the A's where the following season he led the AL in whiffs while hitting .239 in 157 games. A year as a part-timer in 1965 was his omega at only 24. Two.

**6.** At 19 he was the regular first-sacker for the Union Association champs, but for most of the rest of his long career he played second. And did it well. With many clubs, including three separate stints with the Cards, he clocked nearly 1800 hits and finished with the Senators in 1901. Playing experience in four different leagues made him one of only a handful who've accomplished that feat. Three.

**7.** The Braves' infield handy-andy at 19 in 1939, he was a regular the next three seasons but had to wait until 1949 to play in over 100 games again. For some 13 years he played second, third and short with about equal mediocrity—all with the Braves. Two.

**8.** Got your eye out for another grandslammer? Close it, baby, you don't have a chance. This cat put in four seasons behind the bat and at first base for the Yankees before he was 21 and finished in 1914 with a .163 average in 105 games. His most remarkable achievement was being born on Monday in Monday, Ohio.

**9.** I hope that last one left you so stunned you won't click back fast enough to tell me the righty who appeared in six games for the Mackmen in 1943 at 16 and was finished at 27 after playing all or part of 11 seasons. Twice he won in double figures, but his bat always seemed a lot stronger than his arm, and many in Phillie would've liked to see Connie put him in the outfield and leave him there. Such never happened, though, despite his pounding .396 at the plate in 1951 and doing a dismal 1-12 number on the mound. One.

**10.** Easy bingle coming. Who was the 18-year-old the Brewers gave their shortstop job to in 1973? Maybe he's still there, maybe he's not. You want me to tell you everything?

**11.** Going back again to the dim dark 1880s for this 19-year-old phenom who played for his hometown Richmond club in 1884 and showed enough that the Braves took him on when Richmond folded. Showed enough in fact that he held the Braves' third-base post till 1895 with a year out for the Players League caper. He was just about the best glove there was at third in baseball's early years, and his bat wasn't far behind. Two's probably one too many, but my mood's good so run hard.

In 1951 he had a 1-12 pitching record but batted
.396. (Question 9)

**12.** And in our time another 19-year-old phenom hit .310 in 90 games in 1970. He had his 1000th hit by the time he was 25, about the youngest ever to reach that milestone; but many are betting his head won't keep him around long enough to collect 2000. One.

**13.** At 18 he threw two complete winning games for the 1965 Senators—only ten years after his father'd won his last big league game with the Tigers. Still active, our man has had a couple of 20-game seasons with the same Tigers. One.

**14.** Another who was through before he could vote was this oldie first-sacker who saw first daylight at 16 with the White Stockings in 1882, then hooked on regularly with the Wolverines two years later for the first of his three seasons of full-time play. He was dropped by Baltimore after a .190 showing in 1886. Known as "Mikado Milt," he's a grandslam all the way.

*Potential Hits: 14*
*Potential Points: 29*
*Bonus Points: 9*

*(Answers on Page 166)*

# 8TH INNING
## Get Your Z's

*True, some of the boys here are a mite obscure, but knowing the letter their last name begins with should help you to hit this one a ton.*

**1.** One of the Mexican League jumping beans, this Cuban lefty returned to the Giants in 1949 and made NL fans wonder what they did on mounds south of the border when he did such an incredible balk number that he had Leo reeling for the smelling salts. Oddly, though, he somehow managed to fashion a shutout that season before Leo said, "*Adios, amigo.*" One.

**2.** Over the years between 1963 and 1973 this lefty turned in only one complete game in 40 starts, that a shutout with the 1971 Cards, and only two saves in 68 relief appearances. The Astros carried his salary most of the way, but his best toiling was for the 1972 Tigers when he turned in a 1.42 ERA in 22 outings. One.

**3.** An AL loss leader with the 1926 Red Sox, he'd pitched on the Senator flag club two years earlier. Top year was a 9-10 show with the 1923 Nats. Three.

**4.** An effective righty with the White Stockings in the old National Association, "The Charmer" was told good-bye after he turned in a 4-20 performance for the Athletics in the NL lid-lifter. Two.

**5.** His only homer in the bigs isn't in the record books because it came in a game that was rained out before it became official. His career was pretty much of a rainout, despite a snappy start that saw the Indians shell out plenty to acquire his lefty arm from the Browns in 1948. 11-10 that year, he saw no Series action. Swan-songed with an 0-6 record for the 1952 A's. One.

**6.** Cleveland, Washington, the Yanks and the Red Sox all got winning games out of his big right wing. The last came in a relief stint with the 1947 Red Sox, but most of his others occurred in starting roles, albeit infrequent ones over the 11 seasons he wore big league costumes. One.

**7.** His only full season as a regular was as a replacement for Agganis. He came out of it with 27 homers and 93 RBIs but had to wait till 1959 to get another full-time shot. Then with the Nats, he produced 15 homers and a .228 average in 96 games. Another wild swinger whose strikeouts nearly matched his base hits. One.

**8.** Sure, you'd zap Gus Zernial if I tucked him in here, but this AL outfielder from the same era is equally simple. Among the AL's top five hitters in 1948 and again in 1950, he fell off fast after that 1950 show. His only Series came in 1944, though he missed by only a hair playing in another later in his career. One.

**9.** His coda came in 1918 when he saw regular service most of that season at second base for the NL flag winner. Previously a full-time operator for both the Whales and the White Sox, he thus was the only performer in this century to play regularly in the same city for three teams in three different leagues. Even knowing that, you'll still have a tussle to score one here.

**10.** A deuce says you don't recall the Reds' keystone sacker in 1947. It was his only year as a regular, but he had a couple of others as a utility man.

**11.** Your only homer this inning is gift-wrapped in the person of the Dodgers' regular third-sacker in 1911 who said sayonara after a .185 curtain-closer. Five years earlier he'd been nearly as awful in a short tour with the Cards.

**12.** The Orioles liked this bonus-baby backstopper in the late '50s but never well enough to do more than spot him in a few innings here and there. You've got a spot in your column for a triple if you know the boy his pals labelled "Noodles."

**13.** The Senators thought they had their first-sacker of the future when they nabbed this lefty slugger in the 1961 expansion pool, but a .220 average in 118 games over two seasons convinced them otherwise. One.

**14.** The Yankees' leading slugger with six homers as a rook in 1912, he was also the AL's worst fielding outfielder by far and was packed off to the Braves. He finished with the 1915 Terrapins; by then his glove had improved some but not enough to keep him from becoming another of the legion of Federal League blackballers. Three.

**15.** Another trip says you'll miss the rookie Pirate shortstop who hit .300 in 87 games in 1944 and snuck into the NL All-Star team photo that year along with the Pirates' immortal lefty, Cookie Cuccurullo, because the game was played in Pittsburgh and they were used in pre-game practice.

*Potential Hits: 15*
*Potential Points: 28*
*Bonus Points: 0*

*(Answers on Page 166)*

---

9TH INNING
# Not with a Whimper

*Surely you haven't forgotten how this one works. All the performers here had above-average marks and in some cases even super ones in their final bows.*

**1.** This third-sacker played ten seasons in the bigs but waited until his last, with the 1921 Cubs, to post his finest stats—a .289 average and 66 RBIs. Seven years earlier he played in his first Series with the miracle Braves, replacing the injured Red Smith. Three.

**2.** At 27 this outfielder gave the Dodgers a solid .272 season in 1935 after rapping .305 a year earlier. Still, he was sent packing, the owner of a .290 average over five seasons. Two-run homer.

**3.** His first name was Virgin, but this gardener played, naturally, under a nickname—Rip, to be exact. In his second bigtop season, 1905, he played all 154 games for the Braves and was one of their better stickers. The Braves passed on him for 1906, though, and so did everyone else. Homer.

**4.** One of the early top Jewish performers was this old Giant infielder who in two seasons as their regular second-sacker—1928 and 1929—rapped .274 and .294. But when the Giants got Critz from the Reds for the 1930 season, our man became expendable. Two.

**5.** Another Jewish star for the Giants was their backstopper in the '30s who finaled with a .279 in 1942. One.

**6.** Might as well pass this grandslam by. No way you're gonna know the KC Packers' regular right-fielder who over the two Federal League seasons hit a solid .287 and .285 and then was never heard from again.

**7.** At 39 he still had enough to give the Senators some solid shortstopping in 1902 and stroke .262, four points over his lifetime average for 15 seasons. The Pirate's shortstop prior to Wagner, he didn't really become a full-time regular until he joined the Cardinals in 1893 when he was already 30. Four.

**8.** Contract disputes brought an abrupt end to the career of this future Hall of Famer a few years back after he registered a .271 finale in 132 games. Over 18 seasons he poked nearly 2700 hits and swiped over 500 sacks. Easy one.

**9.** Tough three-run homer for the White Sox shortstop who in 1925 scored 105 runs in 146 games in his first and only season as a regular before exiting from the big league arena.

**10.** He won the Dodger second-base job in 1920 in time to play in the Series, and the following year he was rapping .288 when the Bums inexplicably moved Ivy Olson to second near the end of the season and dropped him. Two-run shot.

**11.** Another Dodger who came to the end of the road too early was this third-sacker who gave the Bums a .273 season in 1902 after many fine years before that with the Reds and Cubs. Homer. (Has it occurred to you yet how much higher your average would be if you just knew all the third-sackers the whacky Dodgers employed in the century's first decade or so?)

**12.** Oh, those fickle Bums! They dumped still another regular after the 1927 season, this their left-fielder who gave them a steady .265 season after hitting .280 the year before and rapping .307 with the Braves in 1925. Two-run homer.

**13.** This shortstop sat out the 1921 season after being dealt the previous year to the lowly Phils by the Giants. But in 1922 he bounced back with a .280 finale. In four Series with the Giants, he was one of the NL's top infielders throughout the teens. One.

**14.** The Pirates' regular backstopper in 1917, he pounded out a .286 average in 95 games. Two years before that he'd been the Federal League's batting crown runner-up while catching for the Whales. Only 26 in 1917, he strangely never played again in the bigs despite showing good power and a .274 stick over five seasons. Three.

**15.** Another backstopper to end on. The Reds' first-string mask man for the three years immediately following World War II, he was gone at 29 after going .242 in 127 games in 1948. A sharp drop in power production contributed to the Reds' willingness to surrender his contract, but his backstopping continued to be first-rate to the last. Two.

*Potential Hits: 15*
*Potential Points: 45*
*Bonus Points: 8*

*(Answers on Page 166)*

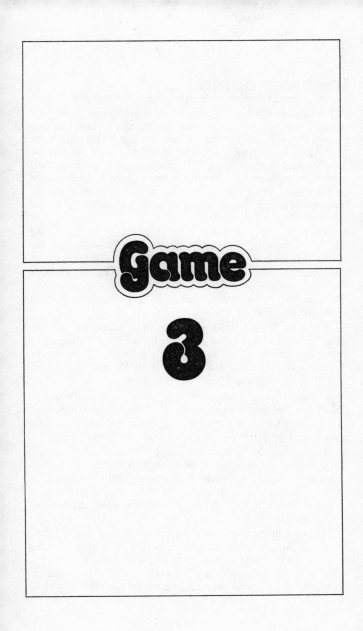

Game

3

# 1ST INNING
# The Unrewarded

**1.** He died in 1952 at 93 after many years in the game as a coach and all-around character, but many by then had forgotten that for nearly two decades in the 19th century he was one of the game's finest third-sackers. With the Browns and Reds most of his playing days, he compiled over 1800 hits and was the first man twice to steal more than 100 sacks in a season. On character alone he probably belongs in the Hall of Fame, but bet plenty that he'll never make it. One.

**2.** Another overlooked early day third-base star, he along with our first man, Deacon White and the Boston great we met in Game 2 were probably the best hot-corner men in the game in the 19th century, yet none is in the Hall of Fame. A .310 stroker lifetime, his best years were with the Philadelphia Association outfit in the 1880s and the Pirates in the 1890s. Two.

**3.** His only Series came with the 1933 Nats, and he responded with a .333 showing. About through by then after being buried away for years in the pasture of the lowly Browns, he last played with the 1936 Pirates. Averaged .292 lifetime in nearly 1200 games. Two.

**4.** Thought of as a wartime star, he was actually better before the war years. Six times he led the AL in thefts, and he consistently hit around .300. Top year was with the 1942 Nats when he pinged .320 and copped 44 bags. One.

**5.** Nobody's touting this outfielder for the Hall of Fame, but he had eight top-notch NL seasons, led twice in triples and was probably the Reds' finest player over the last part of the first decade of this century. Also saw regular duty with the Cubs, Pirates and Nats. One of the real pros of his time. Two.

**6.** He got a bad rap early on because his play around first base was so smooth it looked casual. For over a decade, though, he was one of the AL's top stars. Big year was a .319 with the 1955 A's, but he cleared .300 twice more. Never on a pennant winner, he came closest in 1959,

though it was his double-play hotshot that finally elimi-
nated his club from the AL race. One.

**7.** He'll never make the Hall of Fame, but very few other
third-sackers have matched any of his career stats, much
less all of them. Garnered 2254 hits, 342 homers, 1331
RBIs and 1108 walks, all while playing in the same city.
Never on a pennant winner. One.

**8.** Switched to the outfield when Eddie Collins came up,
he lost a chance at being immortalized as part of the
$100,000 infield. He played on as a regular, however, until
his 35th year. That came in 1911 when he had his best
season, rapping .329 and scoring 104 runs. One.

**9.** Born Jan Smadt, he'd have been a lot better remembered
today if he hadn't chosen to play under another name. A
Card star for years, he was dealt one game into the 1926
season to the Braves and thus missed out on a chance to
play on a pennant winner. A .310 hitter that year, his top
years were in the early '20s when he broke .300 four years
running. Good speed, good arm, he played all three outfield positions well. Three.

**10.** Overshadowed during his playing days by Schalk and
Schang, he usually outhit both of them. His misfortune
was that he didn't get on a pennant winner until his twi-
light years. But then, suddenly, he was on two in a row.
Last game was in the 1926 Series after which he departed at
age 35. Enough clues here for a cinch bingle.

**11.** His arm kept him from ever winning a regular job
with Cleveland. Moving to the Cubs in 1926, he quickly
won their left-field post and wound up in 1934 with a .336
career average, the highest among 20th-century players
who are not in the Hall of Fame—except of course Shoe-
less Joe. One.

**12.** Chances are you've never head of him. Yet for years he
was one of the Association's top catchers and was still good
enough when the upstart league folded to put in a fine year
with Washington in 1892. A .286 hitter lifetime, his top
season was a .366 for the 1889 Browns. Philadelphia clubs
in both the Association and Players League also got fine
years out of him. Three.

**13.** If the George Kellys belong in the Hall of Fame, this
man should be a shoo-in. The last sticker to lead the NL in
hits three years running, he did it his first three seasons as

a regular. His final game came in the 1948 Series. A first-sacker, he was one of the game's top stars for exactly a decade. In easily for one.

*Potential Hits: 13*
*Potential Points: 20*
*Bonus Points: 0*

*(Answers on Page 166)*

---

# 2ND INNING
## Odds and Ends

---

*These puzzlers don't quite fit into any category, but all are so weird and so intriguing they can't be left out. You'll destroy every brain cell you have if you spend too long on any one of them, but each is worth a few moments of work and every base hit will feel like gold.*

**1.** He's seventh among third-basemen on the total games played at that position list, but there came a year early in his career when his club was short a centerfielder and put him out to pasture. All he did that season was lead all NL gardeners in fielding! It happened not that long ago, but two says you'll have forgotten. You need both the man and the year.

**2.** The Pirates got their nickname when they stole this second-sacker away from the Philadelphia Associations after the Players League folded. Name him for two.

**3.** In his ten seasons of activity between 1952 and 1963 he got into 560 games. His top year was 1958 when his name was in 98 boxscores. In those 98 games, though, he only batted 81 official times. That was a typical year for him, as he got up to the plate less than 800 times in his 560 games. The all-time caddy's caddy, utility man's utility man, he made the 1959 Series. Two.

**4.** At 18 he pitched a shutout for the Washington Nationals, at 24 he hit .350 as a Giant outfielder, at 30 he began a string of four seasons in which he caught for and managed the Cards, and at 36 he caught 68 games for the 1915 Cubs. Thirty years later he made the Hall of Fame. His stats are memorable enough to have been included in

In 560 games he came to bat less than 800 times. (Question 3)

any of several different categories, and indeed you've been asked about him before. Not in this book, though, and never in quite this way. Score one.

**5.** A weak stick kept this AL infielder from ever holding a regular job anywhere for very long. He stroked only .222 as the White Sox second-sacker in 1914 and .228 while at short for the Reds four years later. Given his ticket to the minors at 33 after a .213 finale in 1919, he returned eight years later at 41 to slap a run-producing pinch-single; and in 1929, then a player/manager, he chucked a perfect relief bit for the White Sox. Thus he became the only man ever to post a 1.000 batting average and a 0.00 ERA after age 40. Three.

**6.** Dividing the 1904 season between the Pirates and Giants, this rookie gardener got into 125 games and hit .279. Then he disappeared until 1908 when he resurfaced for two seasons, the second as a .292 stick for the Giants. Once more, however, McGraw let him wander away, this time for three years before bringing him back to lead the NL in pinch-raps in 1912. The scorer of the famous run that didn't count in 1908, he's the possessor of one of the weirdest careers ever, and you'll be long-faced if you don't single on him.

**7.** Another weird career belongs to this flychaser who played with six teams in his seven bigtop seasons. A regular with the 1937 Red Sox, he was passed on to the Browns after a .295 showing. The Browns dropped him the next year, despite a .285 follow-up. Brought back by the 1940 Yankees, he hit .397 in 34 games, then amazingly was let go again. Last with Cleveland in 1946, he spread his seven seasons of activity over 13 years and finished with a lifetime .287. Four.

**8.** One of the strangest records is held by this Hall of Fame outfielder who one season scored 133 runs and knocked in only 27. That's a disparity of 106 runs, my friend, and nobody's ever come close to equaling it. One.

**9.** Another hard-to-believe record is held by this fireballing righty who compiled 745 strikeouts in only 693.2 innings of work. He's one of a very few men who've got a K ratio to innings worked of over 1.000, and he's the only one among this select bunch who worked more than 50 innings and never got a single big league start. It ain't Ryne Duren either. One.

**10.** His name appeared in over 100 boxscores, yet he never stepped to the plate a single time. With the new DH rule some AL pitchers have done that feat, but he's the only non-hurler ever to play so often without once getting up to the plate. A little thought will bring one.

**11.** This Card chucker was an NL loss leader in 1902 with 20. Believed to have been born in Boston, he was gone from the big league scene after 1903, and a curious record went with him. He's the only man since 1900 ever to lead either league in a major category about whom not a single firm biographical fact is known. Nobody knows when he was born, when he died, how he threw, batted, looked, any of it. Grandslam.

**12.** Only three men in the 20th century have had seasons in which they hurled over 200 innings and batted over 500 times. A homer for this trio, with the added clue that the one who'll prove toughest performed these two feats 11 years apart. Single for two.

**13.** Excluding pitchers, only two men among the top five fielders lifetime at each of the other eight positions played before World War II. Both curiously are third-sackers, and one incredibly did all that fancy glove-work before 1930. Four for both. One for one.

**14.** This surname can be spelled two different ways. Many big leaguers have played under one spelling or the other, but only four by this name have played more than 400 games. Three are in the Hall of Fame, and the fourth's brother will one day be in the pro football Hall of Fame. What's the name, for one?

*Potential Hits: 14*
*Potential Points: 32*
*Bonus Points: 0*

(Answers on Page 166)

---

# 3RD INNING
# Managerial Meanderings

**1.** Among managers who sat in big league dugouts for more than 200 games, this old Brownie infielder's record for futility stands alone. At the Brownie helm in 1911 and part of 1912, he couldn't even get his charges to play .300 ball. The Reds tried him behind the wheel again in 1937 as a late-season replacement for Dressen and had no thought of retaining him after he lowered his lifetime winning percentage to a record nadir of .287. Our man made the Hall of Fame, but his managerial talents were no factor in his selection. One.

**2.** The manager who compiled the worst record among those in the driver's seat for over 1000 games is this old NL catcher who in eight seasons and part of a ninth between 1934 and 1944 got only .401 play out of his boys. Fifth place with the 1943 Cubs was his high. One.

**3.** Now tell me the name of the only manager to win a pennant in his only year at the helm. It came in 1879 when his Providence charges surprised by beating out the previous year's champs who were managed by his brother. That clue alone makes this only one.

**4.** This former AL shortstop came close to becoming a second man to win a pennant in his only season as a manager when his Red Sox club finished second in 1917. Invited back by the BoSox, he preferred coaching in college. One.

**5.** At the other end of the spectrum we have the luckless skip whose one managerial experience of any length resulted in a 12th-place finish and a .103 winning percentage. You've figured out by now that he was at the Cleveland reins in 1899, but three says you don't click on his name.

**6.** The first manager to win 1000 games is in the Hall of Fame, and his name is not Cap Anson. For one, what is it?

**7.** He played only 19 big league games, but he managed in over 1500. His second season as a helmsman was 1884 when he brought the Baltimore Associations home at .594 and a sixth-place finish. The Baltimores were only 12 games off the pace, however, and though he managed for 12 more seasons or parts thereof, he never came as close to a pennant again. Washington, Louisville and Brooklyn all let him sit a while on their benches in the 1890s. Except for Jimmy Dykes, no other manager has ever sat for so long without winning a flag. Two-run homer.

**8.** Of all the men who have managed in over 1500 games since 1940, only one has never had a losing season. Tough enough for two.

**9.** Another deuce for the first brothers to manage for the same team. Your clue is that one of the two won a World Championship and the other played on a World Champion before taking over the reins.

**10.** He's not in the Hall of Fame, but for years he had the best lifetime winning percentage among skippers in over 2000 games. The producer of five NL pennants in the '90s, he had the Cubs in the thick of things as late as 1905 when he stepped down finally in favor of Chance. One.

**11.** His 1906 Cards played .347 ball and finished 63 games off the pace. Incredibly, that marked his high point, for in three other full seasons at the helm and part of a fourth he never again saw any of his charges do as well as that 1906 bunch. Called "Honest John," he was Louisville's chief when they were the NL dregs in the '90s. Grandslam.

**12.** The first man to win pennants in two different leagues, he skipped the 1883 Mets and the Giant champs in 1888 and 1889. He never played a game in the bigs himself, but when he stepped down in 1891 he took with him one of the all-time finest baseball minds. Two.

**13.** The man most responsible for assembling the White Sox dynasty in the late teens, he preceded Ed Barrow by one year as the first man ever to win an AL pennant without big league playing experience. One.

**14.** Few remember that Boston won the Players League pennant, and fewer still will remember their Hall of Fame skipper. A fabled player, he caused so much trouble for managers and owners alike that it's hard to believe he could have gotten his charges to take him seriously. Somehow he did, though, and if you're serious here you could end with a solid single.

*Potential Hits: 14*
*Potential Points: 25*
*Bonus Points: 4*

(*Answers on Page 167*)

4TH INNING
# Death in the Afternoon

*They went young, and their going in some instances changed the whole course of baseball history as more than one con-*

*tender lost a key man just when about ready to go over the top.*

**1.** As a rook in 1904 this Nat shortstop led the AL in triples. He was in there for every game in 1905, but, alas, he died just a few weeks after his 22nd birthday during the spring training season in 1906. Three.

**2.** Moved to the outfield from second base by Brooklyn midway through the 1891 NL season, he got off to a fast start in 1892 and seemed headed for one of his finest years when he died late in May. The NL's 1890 runs-scored leader, he led the Association in doubles two years earlier. Four.

**3.** This Cub rookie waited a long time to get his big league shot, but when it came in 1911 he was ready. In 130 games he rapped .282 and knocked in 62 runs. Over the off season, however, he died in his Syracuse hometown. Three.

**4.** Pretty much the Pirates' regular third-sacker in 1907, he tried to combine college with a big league career over the next couple of seasons, but it all got away from him when he died before the start of the 1910 season. A Cardinal by then, he also played first and short. Four.

**5.** Slipping a bit after some seven seasons with the Pirates, he came back strong with the Phils in the mid-'20s, winning as high as 17 in 1926. Still an effective chucker with the Cubs as late as 1929, he passed away a few weeks after the season opened. A righty and a good hitter, he was an NL shutout leader in 1925. Two.

**6.** The Phils lost their regular catcher after the 1925 season. Only 26 at the time and coming off his second year in the bigs, he'd shown good power and looked solid for many years to come. Four.

**7.** Another catcher who died too young was this longtime backup man to Schreckengost who'd held the A's regular job all to himself for a time before Connie acquired Oz. Thirty-nine in 1909, he died early in the season not long after catching his final big league game. Three.

**8.** Your eyes are rolling about now, so I'll groove one. A bingle for the Angels' switch-hitting infielder and former LSU quarterback who crashed to his death after the 1976 season. One.

**9.** Back to expert land. This Pittsburgh first-sacker was hitting .340 when he died in 1887. A solid performer for New York and St. Louis for the three previous seasons, he had excellent power. Three-run homer.

**10.** Now that I've got you back there, I'll shoot you another oldie, namely, the fleet Phillie outfielder and ex-stolen-base champ who died after spending the 1890 season in the Players League, where for a few months he managed the Philadelphia entry. Only 27 at the time, his loss was deeply felt by the Phils. Three.

**11.** This big White Sox righty was 1-6 as a rookie in 1969, but the Sox still had high hopes for him. Unfortunately he was gone before the next campaign started. Even Sox fans'll have to think a minute to homer here.

*Potential Hits: 11*
*Potential Points: 35*
*Bonus Points: 2*

*(Answers on Page 167)*

---

5TH INNING
# Who'd They Come Up With?

*Knowing the clothes these stars were wearing the day they first appeared in big league boxscores will jack up your average quickly.*

1. George Foster. One.
2. Jim Gentile. One.
3. Wally Gerber. Three.
4. Cesar Geronimo. One.
5. Bill Madlock. One.
6. Bill Nicholson. Two.
7. Bill North. One.
8. Billy Southworth. Two.
9. Al Spangler. Two.
10. Nels Potter. Three.
11. Steve Hamilton. One.

**12.** Lefty O'Doul. One.
**13.** Hank Majeski. Two.
**14.** Ken Raffensberger. One.
**15.** Both Toothpick Sam and Sad Sam Jones. One.

*Potential Hits: 15*
*Potential Points: 23*
*Bonus Points: 0*

*(Answers on Page 167)*

---

# 6TH INNING
# Rookies

**1.** In 1960 the Orioles chirped when this frosh second-sacker hit .267 in 152 games and swiped ten sacks. The following summer he lost his job to Jerry Adair, however, and never played regularly for the remainder of his four-year career. Two.

**2.** This Phil first-sacker and outfielder hit .287 over 109 games as a rook in 1945. The following year he was hitting .308 after 50 games when the Phils bounced him. Two-run homer, and a guess that even Phil fans will have to ponder this one a while.

**3.** The Indians' rookie gateway guardian hit .292 in 156 games in 1942 before Uncle Sam beckoned. Returning late in 1945, he came in at .329 for 42 games; but in 1946 and again in 1947 he could do no better than alternate for a regular job. A handful of games with the 1949 Pirates was his end. Three.

**4.** Emotional problems kept this Phil first-sacker from living up to his .293 rookie billing in 1957. Later with the Cubs and Mets, he was through after 1962 at only 29. One.

**5.** He wowed Twins fans when he planted 33 balls in the seats in 1963. He had three more seasons after that when he homered 20 or more times, but after 1967 his stroke suddenly deserted him and he began a long downhill trip that saw him trying to hang on with five different clubs. One.

**6.** Earl Smith had a lot of competition for the Pirate catching job from this sturdy switch-hitter in the '20s. As a rook in 1922 our man clubbed .329 in 105 games. Later with the Dodgers, Reds and Red Sox, he was a lifetime .280 hitter over 11 seasons. Three.

7. He set a club mark as a rook in 1934 that stood for 16 years when he rapped 27 homers. It was his best power production, but two years later he knocked in 138 runs; and when he packed it in after the 1940 season, he had a .307 career average. I won't tell you his first club, but you should be able to figure it out. One.

8. In 1940 this Brave frosh clocked 17 homers, 89 RBIs and a .281 average. Though he played four more seasons, his rookie slugging figures were more than half his career totals and his lifetime average was only .241. A major disappointment to the Braves, he'd looked off his rookie stats to be their left-fielder for the rest of the decade. Three.

9. Called "The Flake," he moved from the Cards to the Giants early in 1956 and gave out with a superb .298 lid-lifter before Uncle Sam claimed him. Returning in 1958, he never quite got his act together again, though he hung on into 1967. The Orioles got most of his work; he was their man in center before Blair. One.

10. Yet another who went nowhere after his frosh season was this second-sacker who led the AL in at-bats with the 1928 Indians and hit .294. He held on for two more years but only by the skin of his teeth. Two-run homer.

11. Breaking the pattern for a moment, this old outfielder had many fine seasons after his .343 inaugural with the 1889 Cinci Associations. Moving to the Reds in 1890, he included a .383 in 1894 and a couple of years as a home run leader in his ten-season career. Despite his strong overall stats, however, he was another who was held back some by off-the-field antics. Two.

12. The sophomore jinx didn't phase him; he hit .304 in 1928 after a .319 showing as a rook. But this Pale Hose flychaser slipped fast after that and was released by the Browns after being dealt to them in 1930. Four.

13. It's worth a two-run homer if you know the Phillie yearling shortstop who in 1936 took the field in all 154 games and hit .265. Moved to second in 1937, he vanished after a .257 encore.

14. End with an easy single. The other half of the

Dodgers' rookie tandem in their 1947 infield, he hit .274 in 129 games before losing his job a year later to Cox. Never again a regular, he finished with the 1951 Giants.

*Potential Hits: 14*
*Potential Points: 34*
*Bonus Points: 3*

*(Answers on Page 167)*

---

# 7TH INNING
# Nobody Knows My Name (1920-1929)

---

**1.** In 1926, my second year as the Cards' hot-corner man, I hit .325 and knocked in 100 runs. It was my top season, though I gave the Braves a couple of tough efforts in the late '20s. Wager you a deuce you won't ring my chimes.

**2.** I hung in there from 1915 to 1932, but the '20s were my main years. Just about that whole decade I was the Indians' left-fielder and invariably hit my .300. In 1923 I led the AL in hits and the following year struck .359. Short on power, I left the game ten hits short of 2000. One.

**3.** I'll be a tough homer for you, even though I was twice a .300 hitter for the Phils. With .291 lifetime over seven seasons, I always considered myself one of the NL's better outfielders in those years. Righty all the way, I broke in with the 1921 Pirates and had my best year in 1926 with the Phils.

**4.** It was my fate to be a Yankee in their glory years. Still, in 1925 I got into 89 games and hit .360, and two years later, on the Murderers' Row outfit, I hit .317 as Ruth's caddy. Lifetime I was .309 in 364 games, and Hug himself told me I was the best fourth outfielder a team could want. Four.

**5.** I caught for the Giants, Braves, Pirates and Cards in the '20s and got into five Series. A lifetime .303 clubber, I had my greatest days with the Pirates and for years was a deadly pinch-hitter. In 1926 I hit .346 for the Corsairs and gave McGraw a .336 five years earlier. One.

**6.** My brother broke in with me for the 1922 White Sox, but he quickly dropped out while I went on to give the Pale Hose nearly nine years of solid mound duty. My apex was 1925 when I went 17-8. It was me and Ted and Red for most of those years, and while I'll admit they were better, I wasn't all that far behind. Three.

**7.** In 1922 the Browns just missed winning the flag, and I just missed winning my 20th game. I stayed with the Brownies till 1928 when I went to the Bengals and was still good for 11 wins. Nobody else with my first name ever wore a big league suit. Even with that bit of info, you still get two.

**8.** A grandslam for a guy who averaged .303 over six seasons of play? I think it's way too high, especially when I tell you I played with the A's and my last year was with the 1929 champs. Never much for the long ball, I did get in two years of regular duty before Connie moved Simmons to left in 1928 and me to the bench.

**9.** I'm an easy single. Through the '20s I was the White Sox best hitter and right to the end—with the 1931 Indians—I could still hit .300 with my eyes closed. You couldn't call me the best at my position because I happened to play the same place as Goose, Heinie and Big Al—and you know where they are. But more years than not I was up there close behind them.

**10.** If I'd broken in a year earlier, I would've tied Phil Todt's record for the most consecutive years playing regularly on a cellar dweller. As it was, I got frustrated. I mean I was a pretty darn good second-sacker, and I wasted some nice years with those Crimson Hose before playing out the string with the Pirates. Four.

**11.** Lazzeri made me expendable when he arrived in 1926. Before then, though, I'd been a Yankee regular for six seasons and hit .286 in my three Series. My zenith was 1921 when I slapped .306. Two.

**12.** My bounder that struck a pebble and won the 1924 Series was my high point. A rookie at the time, I went on to play regularly for the balance of the '20s and finished with the Browns in 1931. My .303 in 1926 was my only year of substance, however, and I was at best only an average gardener. The Series clue makes me only a single.

**13.** As the Cubs' centerfielder in 1923 I cracked 209 hits and averaged .319. I had three other seasons of regular play, including 1927 with the Dodgers, but none were quite as good as that one. Mom called me Arnold, but the boys had a name for me that I liked better. Two.

**14.** Though I was around as late as 1935, 1929 marked my last year of regular play. The Dodgers got my best work in the early '20s, but the Braves, Giants and Cubs liked what I did behind the bat too. The Cubs, in fact, caught me in every game in the 1929 Series, my only fall outing. A .310 show for the 1925 Braves was my best. Two.

*Potential Hits: 14*
*Potential Points: 33*
*Bonus Points: 3*

*(Answers on Page 167)*

# 8TH INNING
# Don't Fence Me In

*A quick inning with some of the game's more bizarre sluggers and slugging stats.*

**1.** He had only one full season as an NL regular, in 1910. Yet he led the NL in homers that season; and when the Whales brought him back in 1914 and gave him their first-base job, he took Zwilling down to the wire for the Fed homer crown. Four for this forgotten lefty clubber.

**2.** In yet another way 1910 was an odd slugging year. It was the last season until 1955 that two men playing the same position for teams in the same city won their respective league homer crowns. Like our NL slugger, this AL man never won another; unlike our NL'er, he was right-handed and had numerous other seasons as a regular—though 1911 wasn't one of them. In 1911, in fact, he didn't appear in a single big league game. Two for this weirdie clouter.

**3.** Before Johnny Bench came along, who was the last NL catcher to bang more than 30 homers in a season? Tough single, so I'll throw in the clue that it wasn't Campy.

**4.** Easy single for the clubber who's the only cat to rap over 500 career homers and fan fewer than 800 times.

**5.** Maris fell off some 28 homers the season after his record-breaking performance; but this man, who was also a record-breaker in his own right, fell off 43 homers the year following his fence-busting feat. One.

**6.** Only twice in history have stars rapped over 45 homers and led their leagues in base hits in the same season. With the clues that both men played the same position, that their performances came more than 20 years apart and that it's been over 20 years since it was last done, name both of these sluggers for two. No credit for just one.

**7.** The only slugger ever to rip more than 50 homers in a season and bat under .300 is an easy bingle.

**8.** How about another single for the only swatter to club more than 45 homers and bat under .250 in the same season?

**9.** The last year a homer king failed to connect enough times to get into double figures was 1918. For a deuce, who was the NL rapper that year who led with only eight circuit clouts?

**10.** The Yankees were of course the first AL club to have two sluggers who tagged more than 20 homers in a season. For two, what was the first 20th-century NL club, and who were the two stickers? Need all for credit.

**11.** The only seat-finder to have a season in which he hit more than 35 homers on less than a .235 average brings one.

**12.** The name of the American Association's first swat king in 1882 is worth every inch of a three-run homer.

**13.** When Ned Williamson connected for 27 four-baggers in 1884, whose year-old NL record did he break? Three.

**14.** The first clubber to post a seasonal slugging average over .600 was not Tip O'Neill in 1887 as is popularly believed but another earlier rapper. Historians will reason this one out for an easy double, but the rest of you will have to scramble.

*Potential Hits: 14*
*Potential Points: 27*
*Bonus Points: 2*

*(Answers on Page 168)*

# $9$TH INNING
# Fifties Follies

*A flash of fun and frustration for '50s freaks.*

**1.** For a wicked deuce, who was the lefty for the cellar-dwelling Pirates in 1950 who was second in the NL in saves with eight and went 6-11 as a starter? Called "Bugs," he and Newk were the NL's top rookie winners in 1949, but after 1950 he faltered speedily.

**2.** Albie Pearson wasn't the smallest Senator flychaser in the '50s. That distinction belonged to this ex-Chattanooga star whose 5'4" frame was seen in Nat garb 188 times in 1955 and 1956. Three.

**3.** Remember Jack Cusick who gave the Cubs a fine .171 show as a backup to Smalley in 1951, then rapped .167 behind Logan the following year? If you don't, there's slight chance you'll recall another Jack, this the Brave rookie outfielder up from Milwaukee in 1952 who slugged .187 in 106 games and was never seen up top again. Two.

**4.** The Tigers finished in the basement for the first time in their history in 1952. Jerry Priddy's midseason broken leg pretty well spelled their doom. Three says you can't spell the name of the minor league hoople the Bengals brought up to finish the season at second.

**5.** How about the two Pirate freshmen who alternated at second for the 1952 club? One went .248 in 111 games and the other, who also played a lot of short and third, struck for .261 in 98 games. Neither ever made another hit in the majors, but you'll homer if you know both. Single for one.

**6.** The Orioles escaped the AL cellar in 1954, thanks largely to the garden work of two NL retreads who'd played regularly previously for the Pirates and Cards. The ex-Pirate, in right field, hit .293. The old Card, a fleet center-fielder but a notoriously weak stick, had his finest all-around season since 1949, going .258 and slapping 108 hits. Three for both; zip for only one.

**7.** The name of the smooth-fielding lefty who began the 1954 season as the regular first-sacker for the record-setting Indians is only going for one these days.

At 5'4" this '50s major leaguer was smaller than
Albie Pearson. (Question 2)

**8.** In 1958 Richie Ashburn won the bat crown while playing center for the pack-trailing Phils, but their left-fielder was the real club leader, hitting .301, rapping 23 homers and finishing third in the NL in RBIs. Phillies fans will argue that it's only worth one, and they're right.

**9.** Even rabid Senator fans won't complain when offered two for the lefty swinger who did most of the Nats' work at second base between 1956 and 1958. Now don't embarrass us all and say Pete Runnels who wasn't even with the club in 1958.

**10.** In 1950 he alternated at first with Hopp for the Pirates and hit .293. Six years later he alternated with Torgeson for the Tigers and hit .295. A lifetime .283 hitter, he played little other than those two seasons, though he did go zip for two in the 1947 Series. Three.

**11.** Where were you in 1952? This lefty was on the mound for the Cubs and having his finest season, winning 14 and losing only nine. He was around for a decade, but it's been nearly two since anyone had thoughts of him. Two.

**12.** The name of the Tigers' first-sacker in 1958 and 1959 should be an easy single, especially when you're told he hit 20 homers and knocked in 83 runs in 1958. But I'm guessing you'll go wrong.

**13.** Mike Goliat, we all know, played second for the 1950 Phils. Four goes to any lucky freak who rattles off the two humpties who alternated at second for the 1951 Phils. Generous single for one.

**14.** The Phils used three men in right field in 1954. Wyrostek and Mel Clark were two of them, but the best work was turned in by a big rook who hit .283 in 92 games only to be told to clean his locker after two unsuccessful pinch-hit appearances in 1955. Homer.

*Potential Hits: 14*
*Potential Points: 32*
*Bonus Points: 0*

*(Answers on Page 168)*

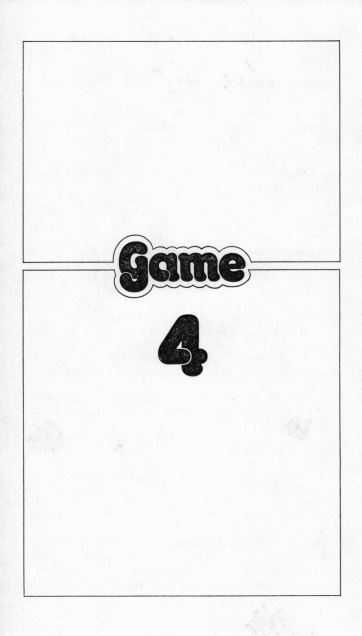

Game

4

# Walking Wounded

*... Some more stars who were either felled early in their careers by injury and illness or able to put it together despite handicaps that would have permanently disabled lesser men.*

**1.** It looked like it was all over for this AL star when he contracted polio in 1955, but he came back to knock in over 100 runs in 1956 and again in 1957. A broken leg in 1958 seemed definitely to spell the end, but once more he battled back to have several more fine seasons. Take away those disabilities and you might have seen a Hall of Fame career instead of a merely great one. One.

**2.** A beanball brought early blindness to this AL slugger of the '30s who had three successive 100-plus RBI seasons for the Browns and Indians before the felling caught up to him. Two.

**3.** A delicate operation saved this lefty's career when a heart attack threatened to end it after it had scarcely begun. The holder of several relief records, he's still going strong. One.

**4.** A rare and often fatal kidney ailment halted this third-sacker's days abruptly in 1970 while he was just reaching his prime. One.

**5.** Asthma brought an early curtain to the play of this AL right-hander who fashioned two 20-game seasons in the mid-'40s. One.

**6.** Another beanball victim in the '30s was this Pale Hose second-sacker whose play dropped off sharply after a .312, 84 RBI season in 1936. Three.

**7.** A withered right arm never stopped this lefty from enjoying three seasons in double figures or from providing some stellar Series' relief work for the Yankees in the early '60s. Amazingly, despite his handicap, he was no slouch at the plate either. One.

**8.** Drink kayoed this Spider star after a .338 debut in 1897. One of the classic examples among the many '90s stars who were knocked off early by the bottle. If he'd lasted a few more seasons, he might have borne the distinction of

Struck out by Old Man Gin. (Question 8)

playing for a club that carried the same nickname as his ethnic extraction. Two.

**9.** Heart trouble finished this Card backstopper in 1961, although he came back a few years later to play a handful of innings for the same team his namesake backstopped for in the 1960 Series. One.

**10.** Another backstopper who had to pack up early because of heart trouble was this ex-Card who hit .300 in 123 games in 1954, his first full season. With the Giants when he was stricken in 1956. One.

*Potential Hits: 10*
*Potintial Points: 14*
*Bonus Points: 0*

(Answers on Page 168)

---

## 2ND INNING
# What Was His Real First Name?

*A breakeroonie....You won't have forgotten how this one goes.*

**1.** Ted Beard. Three.
**2.** Neil Chrisley. Two-run homer.
**3.** Mickey Livingston. Three.
**4.** Smokey Burgess. One.
**5.** Bill Cissell. Four.
**6.** Shano Collins. Three.
**7.** Babe Barna. Four.
**8.** Mickey Witek. Two.
**9.** Buddy Bradford. Two.
**10.** Bake McBride. Two.
**11.** Whitey Witt. One.
**12.** Buster Mills. Three.
**13.** Rocky Bridges. Two.
**14.** Sonnie Siebert. Two.
**15.** Wattie Holm. Four.
**16.** Rip Ripulski. Two.

17. Zeke Bonura. One.
18. Whit Wyatt. Three.
19. Nemo Leibold. Four.
20. Yank Terry. Grandslam.

*Potential Hits: 20*
*Potential Points: 53*
*Bonus Points: 4*

*(Answers on Page 168)*

3RD INNING
# Outstanding Offenders

1. Klein, Ott, Berger and Wilson are thought of instantly when recalling the NL's top sluggers of the early '30s, but for several seasons this Phillie first-sacker was right behind them. In 1932, his peak season, he knocked in a league leading 143 runs, clubbed 24 homers and a .339 average and scored 109 runs. Only 27 at the time, he faded badly the following year and was gone after a disastrous .228 in 1934. Two.

2. Something was going on in 1912 that's never been explained. We all know it was the year Owen Wilson set the all-time triples record, but what is not generally known is that it was also the season the AL triples record was set. For one, what AL star rapped 26 trips that year? Nope, not Wahoo Sam—he later tied the record.

3. In 1948 three Red Sox stars scored over 120 runs, but this Yankee led them all when he crossed the plate 138 times. The clue that although he was 35 at the time he still had enough foot speed left to lead the AL in triples makes this only one.

4. By present-day rules the 1954 AL batting crown would have gone not to Bobby Avila but to another AL star who actually outhit Avila but didn't collect quite enough official at-bats. His total plate appearances, however, were more than enough by current standards. Easy single if you think about those clues.

**5.** Not easy by any means is this next puzzler. For a month of the 1911 season the Browns gave their first-base post to a 28-year-old rook; in return he gave them a .385 average and in the process set the all-time record for the highest lifetime average by a major leaguer who batted more than 60 times. You know this one's a grandslam, but it'd be worth even more to know why no club ever gave this cat a further chance after that meteoric start.

**6.** A dim name today at best, this slugging outfielder was one of the best in his time. In 1899 he was the Cubs' main man; two years later, installed for that one season only at second base, he led the White Sox to the AL's first flag; going over to the Giants for the 1903 season, he was the NL's RBI king and was runner-up for that honor in 1904 and again in 1905. Three says you stumble here.

**7.** Eddie Yost was known as "The Walking Man," but this early day NL outfielder could have put in a claim for the same nickname. His real handle was the same as that of a fabled Revolutionary War hero, and his first team was the hometown Bostons in 1883; but he later played for Providence, the Mets, Cleveland and Washington, among others. Never a great hitter, he had several seasons, as did Yost, in which his walks nearly exceeded his hits, and at one time he held the single season major league record for most bases on balls. Two-run homer.

**8.** In 1948 this Dodger outfielder smacked .327 in 88 games and followed up with a .303 average in 1949 in 74 games. His reward was a ticket to Cinci where after hitting .500 in five games he was dropped. A .317 average in 185 games for this lefty who admittedly wasn't any Speaker in the pasture, but in that era few in the NL were his equal at the dish. Two.

**9.** You modern guys are going to lap up an easy single by telling me the only backstopper since Lombardi to have five .300 seasons.

**10.** This Canadian gardener gave Browning and Orr a battle year after year for Association bat crowns, and twice he actually won. At one time he held the record for the highest one-season average ever in the majors, but an application of modern rules to his stats took that distinction away from him. Two.

**11.** In 1936, his first season as a regular, this Dodger backstopper was the runner-up for the NL bat crown. When he cleaned out his locker for the final time in 1942, he had a .310 average. A Pirate at the time, he also played for the Cubs and Nats. Troubled by a violently fluctuating waistline, he never quite achieved stardom. Two.

**12.** The last two men to rack up five 200-hit seasons in a row did it oddly enough over the same five seasons. The AL'er did it for a frequent pennant winner and the NL'er for a steady cellar dweller. Adding to the parallels, both played most of those years in the same city. Must nail both for one.

**13.** He once had eight successive 200-hit seasons in a row. No one else in major league history has come close. One.

**14.** This 19th-century star once had a season in which he knocked home 121 runs and slugged at a .488 clip. Nothing extraordinary about those stats, you're thinking. Well, our man did it without hitting a single home run! Two bases for naming the all-time top slugging non-slugger.

*Potential Hits: 14*
*Potential Points: 27*
*Bonus Points: 4*

*(Answers on Page 168)*

4TH INNING
# Not with a Whimper

**1.** As the Dodgers' regular third-sacker in 1909 and 1910, he led the NL in fielding both years, thus breaking a long string of dismal Dodger hot-corner work. Even so, in keeping with the Dodgers' zany operation, he was dropped and did not reappear as a regular until 1914 when the Pittsburgh Rebels gave him a job. That year all he did was show himself to be the Feds' top third-sacker and one of the league's best hitters. His reward was a spot behind Mike McNally on the Rebels' bench for 1915, his last season. Even then, he made it a good one, leading the Feds' in pinch-hits and hitting .302 overall. One of the classic buried careers, this New Jerseyite could do it all—and proved it on those rare occasions when he got the chance. Four.

**2.** At .279 as a rook second-sacker for the 1908 Red Sox, he finished a .280 campaign as the Pale Hose keystoner in 1911. Those were his top two years, but he looked capable of many more. Homer.

**3.** A grandslammer for the name of the Cinci Associations' centerfielder who departed after a .318 finale in 1886. He'd had good years previously for the Browns and broke in with Boston in 1881. A switch-hitter, he lived till his 87th year.

**4.** Another switch-sticker who exited prematurely was this Cleveland gardener who gave them a solid season in left in 1904 after a fine 1903 effort with the Tigers. Also a regular previously with the Braves and the Washington Nationals as far back as 1896, he was a good baserunner and was just starting to get it together as a hitter when he went. Two-run homer.

**5.** He was supposed to fill Gehringer's shoes but was dealt to the A's when it began to look like Charlie would go on forever. Had two seasons as a regular for Connie, but his last, in 1941, was his finest. In 141 games he hit .271 and tagged eight homers. Thought for a time to be one of the game's coming stars, World War II interrupted his career, and he never returned to the majors. Two.

**6.** Tough inning, eh? Try this oldie outfielder about whom little was known despite a solid 12-year career. Finished with a .276 outing for the 1890 Philadelphia Association club. A .316 in 1889 was his top show, but he had good marks before then for the Redlegs, Buffalo and the Philadelphia Nationals. William was his name, but he played under the same monicker as a later-day Giant shortstop. Three-run homer.

**7.** His bat work for the Braves slipped to .253 in 1936 after a .303 the previous year, but he remained one one of the NL's best defensive left-fielders and looked still in his prime at 31. His first regular effort resulted in a .303 with the 1932 Phils and included a career-high 18 homers. Known as "Sheriff," he'll net you two.

**8.** A star for the Browns, Tigers and Red Sox from 1921 through 1933, he divided his field time about equally between third and second. Moving to the Braves in 1934 after two seasons as the BoSox playing skipper, he was still sharp enough to hit .276 in 119 games. The AL steal champ in 1930, he was at his best while a Brownie. One.

**9.** He hit a solid .281 for the Giants in 1903, but McGraw gave the Giants' third-base job to Devlin the following spring and dispatched him. Only 29 at the time, he'd been the Phils' regular hot-corner man in the late '90s and one of the NL's better ones. Four.

**10.** The White Sox brought this former Red Sox first-sacker from the early '40s back for a final bow in 1948, and he made it a good one—playing in every game and leading the Sox in steals and all AL first-sackers in fielding chances. Never long on power, he was a real swiftie on the bases and had a .283 season as a Phil regular in 1944 before a sojourn in the minors where the White Sox found him. Two.

**11.** Only 30 in 1893, he put away his first-sacker's mitt after a .317 coda with the Washington Nats. Long a solid .300 hitter, he had his best years with the Philadelphia Associations and managed the Cleveland Players League entry for a time. A .303 rapper with over 1400 hits, he was in his day one of the Association's top sluggers, but you'll need an expert's wand to conjure up a homer here.

**12.** The Reds retrieved this second-sacker from the minors at age 32 in time for the 1919 season, and he gave them two years of fine work, ending with a .267 in 129 games in 1920. A regular almost a decade earlier with the White Sox, he was born in the thriving metropolis of Mobeetie, Texas. Three.

**13.** Despite being the Cubs' top hitter and run-producer in the 1938 Series, this gardener was packed off to the Phils in 1939 and suffered a dismal season. Both 1940 and 1941 were decent years, however, and he seemed at 28 to be good for a long while yet. But a service interruption ended it for him. Coast League fans won't have forgotten this rapper. Two.

*Potential Hits: 13*
*Potential Points: 40*
*Bonus Points: 6*

*(Answers on Page 169)*

# Hose

**1.** Only one man in major league history has won 20 games in a season while working in fewer than 200 innings. Adding the clues that he did it as a rookie, was the AL's top reliever in 1957 and won his last game in Cardinal garb at age 30 in 1960 makes it only one, kid. Thinking-cap time, because this one's guaranteed to win a lot of bar bets.

**2.** This tall lefty took the mound 421 times between 1961 and 1972 and 17 of those outings were starts. Yet overall he worked in only 663.2 innings, making his appearances-to-innings-pitched ratio about as low as you can go and far and away the lowest among hurlers in over 400 games who made at least one start. The Yanks, Nats, Giants and Cubs all got good mileage out of him. One.

**3.** Now, what about the hurlers in over 400 games who didn't make any starts? Well, there was a lefty between 1963 and 1975 who toed the rubber 444 times and wound up with only 522 innings. They could've called him "Third of an Inning _____," because that was about his limit. With the Cards, Phils, Astros, Royals and Braves he managed 91 saves. In 1968, his acme, he went 8-2 with 18 saves in only 49 innings; that comes out to better than a save or a decision for every other inning of work. Talk about getting mileage out of an arm, the Cards that season got the absolute max out of this cat. One.

**4.** The AL's save leader in 1975, he was 7-0 in relief as a rook in 1972. Despite an 0-6 career record as a starter through 1975, he was moved out of the bullpen and put into the regular rotation for his club in 1976. Remember what happened to Ike Delock when he was made a starter? This big righty looked like another Ike, for he was 9-17 in 1976. Back in the bullpen in 1977, though, he had a super season. One.

**5.** One of the truly odd careers belonged to this Senator southpaw who over nine full seasons between 1927 and 1935 averaged only slightly more than nine decisions a year and never once either won or lost in double figures. His workhorse campaign was in 1934, when he went 8-8 in 168 innings and had seven complete games. You won't find anyone who labored for so long in the bigs with so little to show for it in the way of career stats. Racked up 38-46 lifetime with only five saves. Four.

**6.** This lefty won 17 for the Red Sox in 1946 and seemed about ready to take the mantle of being the AL's top southpaw away from Newhouser. He slipped horribly thereafter, however, and was handed cheap to the Senators in 1949. A year later, out of nowhere, he suddenly emerged as the AL's top bullpenner, leading the league in both appearances and saves. That performance proved as illusory as his 1946 effort, though, for after putting in the 1952 season as a mopup man for the Indians he was gone. One.

**7.** The Giants' workhorse starter in the late '30s, he was the NL's workhorse reliever for the Reds a decade later. In 61 games in 1948 he went 10-8 with 17 saves. Then 39, he didn't have much left, but he was around long enough to win 143 times and get into three Series, two of them with the Cards. Single.

**8.** In 1961 at 22 he led the AL in shutouts, two seasons later he won 20, and in 1967 he teamed with Stu Miller to pitch one of the strangest no-hitters of all time. Yet, withal, his career was a disappointment, and though he hung on into the 1974 season, everyone had pretty much forgotten by then that after his early promise he'd looked like the AL's king southpaw for years to come. One.

**9.** Nothing tricky about this one. Just a pretty fair country pitcher whom time has passed by. A 23-game winner with the 1901 Cards, he equaled that total with the Reds in 1904, the year he also led the NL in shutouts. Those were his vintage years, and you'll have a vintage two-run shot if you zap him.

**10.** The last man to lose as many as 27 games in a season, he did it in 1933. It was the only year he lost 20, but he had four seasons after that as a 20-game winner, including 1939 when his 25-7 was almost the exact reverse of that 7-27 debacle six years earlier. One for this 223-game winner who was in four Series for the NL.

**11.** The first two arms to work more than 65 games in a season, they did it in the NL during World War II. The first, a Giant, went to the hill 70 times in 1943 and was 11-7. He's still well remembered today, but his Phil counterpart, who was 9-8 in 67 outings in 1945, is not. Hence you need both for a triple.

**12.** The name of the Pirate righty who in 1930 became the only chucker ever to lead his league in wins while posting an ERA over 5.00—5.02, to be exact—scores a deuce.

**13.** You can be proud of yourself if you nail this two-run shot. Just fill in the names of the only two hurlers who won ERA crowns in the NL both before and after 1894—the first season the mound was at its present 60' 6" distance from the plate. This feat becomes all the more remarkable when you take into account how many hill careers were brought to an abrupt end by that rule change. The clue that one of them's in the Hall of Fame won't help you much to nail the second man, and you need both to score here.

**14.** Fifteen chuckers won 20 or more games in the Federal League, but only one man did it both years the Feds were in operation. Even with the info that he later won in double figures for both the Cubs and Cards, you're still a longshot to score a homer on this one.

*Potential Hits: 14*
*Potential Points: 29*
*Bonus Points: 2*

*(Answers on Page 169)*

---

6TH INNING
# Teen Terrors

---

**1.** He got off the mark quickly when he racked up ten wins in 1970 before his 20th birthday. He's got over 100 under his belt now, but he still seems short of arriving at his full potential. With his second club at the moment, after a lengthy and bitter salary dispute with his first. One.

**2.** Another hill man who started early was this Senator lefty who threw his first slants up to AL hitters in 1913 at age 18. In 1916 he was 15-10 but he led the AL in losses three years later and put his burned-out wing away for keeps after a single unsuccessful start with the Bums in 1923. Three.

**3.** The Astros had a long love affair with this outfielder, giving him many chances despite his repeated flops. Starting in 1965 at 19, he played off and on for the next ten seasons and wound up with the Braves as the owner of a .238 average in 540 games. A regular only in 1969. One.

**4.** Before his 20th birthday he was playing short for the Tigers in 1942. But the war cut in on him, and it wasn't until 1948 that he returned to stay. Top year was 1950 when he scored 104 runs to go with his .293 average. Later saw duty at short for the Red Sox. One.

**5.** Still around when he was 39, he got off the launching pad at 18 when he hit .381 for the 1934 Cubs in seven games. A regular for the next three seasons, he went into eclipse for a while before emerging during the war as an NL star. Hit .317 in three Series and played some 22 years in Chi. Simple one, eh?

**6.** Not so simple, though, is this next "Dashing Dan" who at 18 was pinch-hitting for the 1913 Yankees and two years later led the NL in pinch-swats for the Pirates. Through a year later after putting in some spot outfield work. Somehow I can't rouse myself to give a grandslam for a guy who was once a league leader, so try for a three-run shot.

**7.** Another catcher who was playing at a tender age was this hometown boy who in 1944 at 18 rapped .375 in a short look for the Indians. The kid could swat—he homered three times in 1947 in only 27 at-bats—but his mask work wasn't the greatest, and somehow he drifted away after that season, still a few months short of casting his first ballot. Another blast with the sacks jammed for the Poles' boy wonder.

**8.** Spare me the nonentities, you're saying. Okay then, tell me the outfielder named after the guy Rutherford B. ran against who was a Dodger regular at 19 in 1898 and three years later led the NL in slugging and triples while slapping .353 for the Bums. He moved to the Cubs in 1906; and although his bat had slipped some by then, his base running prowess hadn't. He was tenth on the all-time stolen base list until Joe Morgan caught him in 1976. Single only; you wanted an easy one, so don't expect the moon to come with it.

**9.** At 19 he pitched a shutout for the 1915 Pirates, but he was nearly 30 before he made it into the bigs to stay. With

A big bonus and lots of freckles didn't help this man stay in the majors. (Question 11)

the Pirates in 1927 he won 22 and added 16 a year later before running out of steam. One of the first to pitch with specs on. Two.

**10.** This was the man many in the Met organization thought would one day be their first Hall of Famer. Still short of his 20th birthday, he hit .290 in 11 games in 1965. Over the next five seasons he played for the Mets, Pilots, Brewers and Senators, dividing his hours between the mask and first base. Big, with good power, he hit ten homers for the Pilots in 1969, but like the man you're going to meet next he never quite grew into the shoes that were fitted for him as a teenager. One.

**11.** Big bucks were stuffed into his pockets by the Browns. Uncle Sam took him away for two years after he played a few dozen games for Veeck's charges in 1952 at 19, and when he returned in 1955 he was dealt to the Tigers. Tried and found wanting over three seasons in the Motor City, he moved on later to the Indians, Cards and Senators. Mainly a catcher, he played the outfield and first base too, swatting .228 in 229 games. He had a lot of freckles, and maybe they were some of what charmed the Browns into parting with a wad of their slim bankroll. Two.

**12.** This Texan is still around, so the clues'll be scant. The hoopla that attended his mound debut in 1973 when he was 18 would've done credit to MGM. He managed, despite it all, to win four games that year and three the next, but he's still looking to put a major league act together. One.

**13.** Gotta end with this boy who at 16 was playing short for the Dodgers in 1944 and who was all through at 25 after a Cub trial in 1953 that made Bruin fans yearn for Smalley's arm—which could be counted on to find Fondy's glove at least occasionally. That nickname "Buckshot" wasn't an idle one, my friend, for the kid could've been a tough hitter if he hadn't had to worry all the time whether his next throw was going to decapitate somebody in about the tenth row back. One.

*Potential Hits: 13*
*Potential Points: 23*
*Bonus Points: 5*

*(Answers on Page 169)*

# Travelin' Man

*These boys got around. For a variety of reasons none of them stayed put for more than a year or two, and some changed uniforms so often they appeared sometimes in as many as three or four team pictures in the space of a single season.*

**1.** Starting with Washington in 1899 and ending in 1908, a season he split between the Cards and Giants, this old outfielder played with seven NL clubs. Only with the Phils did he settle down long enough to show what he could do. In 1902-03 he was a solid fixture beside Roy Thomas. But then the merry-go-round began again, and he was passed quickly to the Cubs and then on to the Reds. Just so, in 1905, dividing his time between those last two teams, he stroked .304 in 152 games and scored 100 runs. Card and Brave fans also saw a fair amount of him. Besides being a traveler, he was also quite a jack-of-all-trades, playing all four infield positions at times and handling the Reds' first-base slot for most of 1905. Three.

**2.** What his school days were like nobody knows, but his baseball days found him playing in the Association, NL and Players League between 1883 and 1898. The owner of one of baseball's all-time great outfield arms, he could hit (.321 for the Boston Associations in 1891 and a league leading 177 runs scored) and scoot too (both an NL and Association leader in stolen bases at times). With Boston clubs in all three leagues, he was also with Columbus, Pittsburgh, Indianapolis, Louisville, St. Louis and Washington. The compiler of nearly 1900 hits, he scored almost as many runs as Nap Lajoie over his long career. And you'll score two for his name.

**3.** This modern traveler was with his eighth club in 1977. As a regular outfielder and DH, he's hit as high as .329 and as low as .239. Dick Allen gets the attention as the man no manager can handle, but our swatter runs him a close second. One.

**4.** The Mets liked him enough to make him their top pick in the NL expansion draft, but soon sent him to the Orioles who in turn packed him off to the Senators. Before joining Casey's shock troops he played with the Reds, Cubs, Cards and Giants and actually stayed long enough in some of those places to catch regularly. The expansion bit makes this only worth one.

**5.** After playing five seasons for the Yankees—two-and-a-half of them as their regular shortstop—he went to the Red Sox in 1934 and thus began the whirlwind that saw him over the next seven seasons with six different clubs, including two stints with the Browns and a couple of solid seasons as Boudreau's predecessor. The AL's stolen-base champ in 1936, he was a steadying influence everywhere he went despite his battered suitcase. One.

**6.** He played the outfield uninterrupted for the Browns in the late '40s; but after rapping .309 in 114 games for the A's in 1950, he quickly began earning his nickname "Gulliver." In 1951 he tied the major league record when he played with four different AL clubs, and a year later found him with still a fifth. Problems curtailed his career just when it seemed about to blossom. One.

**7.** In Series action with the Indians and later with the Yankees, he rapped .348. Three years in a row in the early '50s he knocked in over 100 runs, and in 1951 he tied Zernial's year-old White Sox homer record. Also with the Orioles, Tigers, Senators and A's in both Phillie and KC, he saw action in every AL port except Boston in his 13 seasons. One.

**8.** He played the outfield for seven clubs between 1934 and 1946, but his frosh season with the Cubs—when he hit .304 in 104 games—was both his most fertile and most active. Still, he was pretty much a regular with the 1945 Yankees and again with the A's in 1946. Also with the Cards, Dodgers, Phils and Tigers, he got into two Series and remained a well-known name on the baseball horizon for years despite his erratic and irregular play. Three.

**9.** The game's early years were replete with merry-go-round backstoppers, and this New Yorker was typical. With seven clubs, he played over 1000 games and was at two separate junctures the Giants' regular mask man. Also played a lot for Louisville, the Red Sox and the Nats. Big years were in 1897 and 1898 when he caught 110 games on each occasion for Bill Joyce's men. Four.

**10.** Seven different clubs got winning games out of him, and the Browns had him in 1939 when he led the AL in losses. Three years earlier he won 21 for the White Sox. 1943 was his last good outing when he won ten for the Indians, but as late as 1945 he still had enough muscle left to work nearly 200 innings with the Phils and Reds. One of the game's better hitting moundsmen, he never—despite all that traveling—got on a pennant winner. Two.

**11.** So well known as a traveler is this next lefty that he's only worth one. His 83 career decisions were spread out over ten different uniforms; Pittsburgh got 38 of them in the mid-'50s, but the Browns got a sizable chunk too earlier on. The Cubs, Cards, Braves, Giants, Orioles, White Sox, Red Sox and Tigers all let him put his toe on their rubber just about long enough to get it soiled.

**12.** Well, I know you got the last man. This next southy from the same era may prove a little tougher, but he's still only worth one. Cleveland had him first but couldn't find room for him and pushed him along to the White Sox where he won ten in 1949. After that the Senators, Yankees, Orioles, Phils, Pirates and Cards had him, and only the Bombers liked him enough to keep him a full season. Nearly four, in fact. One of the Yanks' main spot starters in the early '50s, you may remember him more for his bullpen work.

**13.** Oh, he's in the Hall of Fame all right, but it took him a long time to get there considering he won 270 games and three more in Series' action. One of his problems was that those 270 wins were spread among seven different uniforms. The first came with the Pirates in 1916 and the last with the Yankees in 1934. The Yankee win was the only one in the AL, but he won at least three games for every NL club except the Reds and Phils and had three separate stints with the Pirates and two with the Cards. The Dodgers got most of his best years, but the Pirates had him for his biggest—25 wins in 330 innings in 1928. One.

**14.** A homer to end on? Sure, just name the outfielder who began with the Phils in 1901 and wound up with them in 1912. The years between saw him with the Giants, Braves, Cubs, Nats, White Sox and Dodgers; and for a good number of them, particularly under McGraw, he was one of the best. The NL leader in runs scored in 1904, he stroked .313

the previous year. Sounds like you should get him, doesn't it? Bet?

*Potential Hits: 14*
*Potential Points: 26*
*Bonus Points: 0*

*(Answers on Page 169)*

---

# 8TH INNING
# Wine for Water

**1.** Johnny Evers bumped this longtime NL star off the Cubs' second-base post in 1902. For two, who was he?

**2.** Hornsby played several seasons at short and third before claiming the Cards' second-base slot in 1920. For a medium-range triple, who was the .307 hitter in 1919 who swapped positions permanently with the Rajah for the 1920 season?

**3.** Mantle's showing in spring training in 1951 made Stengel move this star to the bench. With the clue that he didn't stay on the bench for long and the caution to think a bit about this one before committing yourself, you should slap a bingle.

**4.** Clemente took over the Pirates' right-field job for many years to come in 1955. Single by telling me the .306 hitter he replaced.

**5.** Goody Rosen smacked .325 in 1945 but gave way in centerfield the following season to this Dodger rookie who went on to star for over a decade. Look both ways before you bunt for a single on this one or you're liable to be decked from behind.

**6.** What future Hall of Famer took Barry McCormick's job when Mac jumped to the Browns for the 1902 season? Two.

**7.** Joe Judge anchored the Nats' infield for nearly two decades. Go you for a deuce you can't name the gateway star he replaced for the 1916 season.

**8.** Grandslam for the cat Speaker replaced in centerfield for the Red Sox after the 1908 season. One of the least remembered regulars ever to perform in the AL, he vanished forever from public view after leaving the game, and word of what happened to him is worth plenty to historians.

**9.** Whose place did Traynor take when he became the Pirates' third-sacker in 1922? Two.

**10.** Brooks Robinson wasn't filling the shoes of just anyone when he took over the Orioles' hot corner for keeps in 1958. The name of his predecessor will bring you one.

**11.** Tiger fans might know whom Gehringer took the Bengals' second-base job away from for the 1926 season, but few others will score four here.

**12.** Another caution to walk slow comes to you before I ask what Hall of Famer Bob Elliott replaced as a rook in 1939. One.

**13.** In 1927 he hit .331 for the Giants but lost his right-field job to Mel Ott the following season. Two years later he hit a solid .291 as the Braves' left-fielder but was intimidated into an early retirement by the approaching footsteps of Wally Berger. For two, nail down this star who was jostled aside so rudely by these two NL greats.

**14.** In 1932 Stinky Davis made his debut in the AL with a .269 average and 74 RBIs. Not bad; but he had absolutely no chance of holding on to his job when this Hall of Fame rook boomed on the scene early in 1933, and it was four years before the Stinker recovered enough from his shock to return to the majors with the Browns. One.

*Potential Hits: 14*
*Potential Points: 27*
*Bonus Points: 3*

*(Answers on Page 169)*

# 9TH INNING
# Nobody Knows My Name (1930-1939)

**1.** The Yanks liked me well enough to play me in 92 games as a rook in 1930. It was with the Red Sox, though, a couple of years later, that I found my home. My switch-hitting brought me regular garden duty for a time, though in later years I never quite matched my 1933 marks when I hit .291 and slapped ten triples. I'll add that I finished with the 1938 Reds, but I'm still a homer.

2.  From 1935 through 1937 I was the Reds' second-sacker. Once they got Frey, though, they passed me over to the Giants who gave me a lot of action in 1938 but lost interest a year later. A model of consistency, I hit .249 three years in a row and was a lifetime .243. Three.

3.  The Indians had one of the top shortstops in the game in the middle '30s—namely me. In my three years for them I hit .317, .298 and .294. Moving to the Browns in 1937, I was never the same player again and went on to play in utility roles for the Yankees, White Sox and A's before calling it quits. One.

4.  Yeah, well, that shortstop wasn't the only unheralded star the Indians had in those years. You're forgetting that I was their backstopper and a damn good one. I didn't hit hard, but I hit often—.321 in 1936, .315 in 1937 and .308 in 1938. Feller liked me, and so'd the Red Sox for whom I caught later on. Two.

5.  I debuted with a .304 for the Phils in 1934. A second-sacker at the time, I later played regularly at third and in the outfield. The Giants got some good work when they swapped for me in 1937, but the Phils had my three best years. Three.

6.  The Pirates liked my backstopping and especially my bat. The Phils, who acquired me before the 1936 season, weren't as impressed, and after two years with them I was asked to take a hike. My top show was a .274 in 1932 in 115 games, though I was .289 a year later in 12 fewer games. Four.

7.  I might be your easiest grandslam. The Phils' main second-sacker in 1931 and again in 1932, I was released after that. Bobbing up with the Bees in 1934, I gave them a .274 swan song a year later as their regular at second. With a .283 lifetime, I'd like to think at least a few of you haven't forgotten me.

8.  The fact that I was a Gas Houser and a good one makes me only a single. I had a year as a regular in 1929, but it was my play from 1932 through 1934 that I'm proudest of. In 1932 I hit .336, a year later .298 and then .300 in 1934.

Lifetime I came out at .306 and played in four Series, all with the Birds. Ducky had no complaints when he played beside me.

**9.** The Phils, Dodgers, Pirates and Cubs all gave me the mask and let me work. The Pirates got my best shot, a .307 in 1937 in 133 games, but I was .318 three years earlier with the Phils. Though I played 11 seasons, I never got into a Series. One.

**10.** Everybody liked my glove, but my bat was something else again. I played first string for the Red Sox, A's and Bees but never once broke .250. Short was my favorite spot, and the Bees got my best work there in the late '30s. Stand-up double.

**11.** The A's gave me some first-team work at short and second in the early '30s, and the Red Sox tried me all around the infield as late as 1935. But in 1931, my only Series year, I played short in all seven games against the Gas Housers and hit .320. Four.

**12.** A lame wing kayoed me after I won 19 for the 1938 Cubs and led the NL in strikeouts. I was good for only two wins after that, but knowing that I later managed for a long time in the Dodger chain will get you in for one if you've forgotten my 1938 stats.

**13.** How they can rate me a two-run homer I'll never know. After all, I was one of the NL shutout leaders in 1935 while winning 14 for the Pirates, a victory total I repeated the following year. I also pitched for the Browns, Yankees, Senators, Cubs and Reds and had a winning record every year I registered a decision. And I wasn't bad coming out of the bullpen either.

**14.** When the Tigers got Cochrane, I went to the bench of course. Before Mick came along, though, I had four solid seasons as a Bengal regular and played first string again for a while in 1936 after he got beaned. I was still around as a bullpen operator with the Dodgers during the war—the same years, I should tell you, that my kid brother was catching for the Browns. Two.

*Potential Hits: 14*
*Potential Points: 36*
*Bonus Points: 4*

*(Answers on Page 170)*

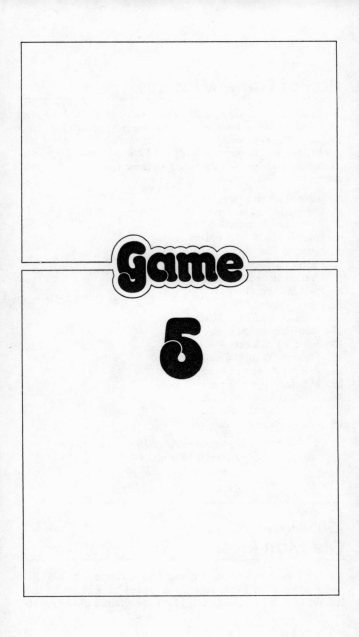

Game

5

# Hall of Fame Middlers

*Tyrus Raymond, George Herman, Grover Cleveland—the first and middle names of this trio are almost inseparable. But how about the middlers of some of these other greats? No tricks here, no Hornsbys who didn't have a middle name; all these boys had true middlers and in some cases quite famous ones.*

1. Jesse Burkett. Two.
2. Walter Johnson. One.
3. Aloysius Szymanski. Four.
4. Joseph Medwick. Three.
5. Gordon Cochrane. Two.
6. Frank Chance. Three.
7. Dennis Brouthers. Four.
8. Paul Waner. One.
9. John Wagner. Two.
10. Lucius Appling. Three.
11. Jack Robinson. One.
12. Fredrick Clarke. Four.
13. Denton Young. One.
14. Adrian Anson. Three.
15. Monford Irvin. Four.
16. Edward Collins. One.
17. Harry Hooper. Three.
18. Leroy Paige. Two.

*Potential Hits: 18*
*Potential Points: 44*
*Bonus Points: 0*

*(Answers on Page 170)*

# Ole Man River

1. The Senators couldn't quite find a home for this 30-year-old rook in 1894, so they shuttled him between the infield and the outfield. Still, he gave them a .322 season

with 90 RBIs. Dealt to Louisville late in 1895, he tailed off and was gone a year later. Known in the record books as "Roaring Bill," but old Washington fans remember him as "Wild Bill," and off his rookie year he was well remembered for quite some time indeed. Three-run homer.

2. He was 31 before he won his first big league game with the 1942 A's, and he knocked off 20 with the Nats three years later. A knuckleball specialist, one of his last starts was for the Pirates in the famous ten-homer game against the Cards in 1947. Two.

3. He appeared in a handful of games with the 1938 Yankees, but it wasn't till 1940, when he was in his 30th year, that he stuck with the Reds. That year he led all NL relievers in wins and saves and was still tough as late as 1947 after moving over to the Giants. Primarily a starter in 1946, he was 12-10 that year. Two.

4. Another 20-game winner who didn't come up to stay till he was past 30 was this ex-Dodger who entered the charmed circle in 1939 after being in double figures for the Bums the two previous seasons. Last seen in 190 innings for the 1944 A's, he contributed to the 1941 NL flag team. One.

5. You '50s fans will score an easy one for the 33-year-old Cuban righty who arrived with the Nats in 1950. Around for five seasons and 39 wins, he had some of the most God-awful junk deliveries ever seen in the majors but still found his way to seven shutouts. One.

6. The AL's leader in saves in 1927, he also made 12 starts in that his rookie season and posted 19 wins. Thirty at the time, he stuck till he was 36 and repeated as the AL save leader with the 1931 Red Sox. 2-0 in Series action. You shouldn't need his original club to bingle.

7. Inside-the-park homer for this old Phil, Red and Cub righty who first saw big league light in 1910 at 30, led the NL in winning percentage in 1913 and in 1915, his final year, was still tough enough to post a 2.31 ERA in 171 innings.

8. Nothing was wrong with this chucker's career, except that it didn't get started till he was 31. Still around as late as 1946 when he was then 43, he split his 158 career wins among four NL clubs. Most of his decisions came with the Dodgers, but he won 22 for the 1939 Cards and was good for 19 as a Phil rook. One.

**9.** Another Cuban righty who threw his first bigtop ball for the 1950 Nats was this 30-year-old junker who went on to lead the AL in winning percentage in 1954 for the Pale Hose. Posted a solid .614 lifetime winning percentage, including a neat 6-0 in 1952. One.

**10.** He got in a few games in the teens with three different clubs but didn't post his first win till his 30th year in 1920 when he was 18-12 for the Browns. Solid for the Brownies over the next six seasons, he was an AL shutout leader in 1924. Control trouble was part of the reason for his belated start, and the problem continued to plague him all through his career. Three for this lean righty.

**11.** The Pirates gave this flychaser a shot in the early '40s, then they let him go. Returning to the bigs at 32 with the 1948 Yankees, he was quickly swapped to the Nats where he was the AL's runner-up in triples that season. Still with the White Sox as late as 1954, he had only three years as a regular—all for the Nats—but was a solid spot player and pinch-hitter to his last at-bat. Two.

**12.** A Nat rookie at 22 in 1955, he saw action in their bullpen that year and again in 1957. But he proved so ineffective that it wasn't till 1963, at age 30, that he returned to the bigs and posted the first of his 148 career saves. An Indian then, he later worked with devastating effect for five other clubs. One.

**13.** Thirty-two before he scored his first win in 1939, he nailed down his 143rd ten years later. All came in the same uniform, and though he never pitched in a Series, he threw up a serving once in All-Star competition that they're still talking about. Twice a 20-game winner, he finished with a .596 winning percentage, although his club rarely broke out of the second division. One.

**14.** End as a champ and tell me the righty who came aboard as a 30-year-old rook with the above man's club in 1938. An NL loss leader in 1939, he later became an effective reliever and was an AL save leader with the 1946 Red Sox. Still tough in spot roles the following year, he lost two seasons to Uncle Sam. Two.

*Potential Hits: 14*
*Potential Points: 26*
*Bonus Points: 2*

(*Answers on Page 170*)

# 3RD INNING
## Rookies

**1.** Our best since Gehringer, Tiger fans were saying after he led the AL in triples and swiped 30 sacks in 1961. A Gehringer he wasn't in the field, however; and when his bat slipped in 1962, he became a part-timer. Finished with the 1967 Reds. One.

**2.** KC fans were delighted when he came in with a 12-1 season and a 2.06 ERA as a frosh in 1966. A year later he won 12 again, but the difference was he also lost 17. He was around through 1972 and had several decent seasons, but none came remotely near his lid-lifter. One.

**3.** Another AL hurler who started off fast in the late '60s was this Angel righty who was 12-11 in 1968. His arm was never quite right after that, and he called it quits after 1972 with only 19 career wins. Two.

**4.** As long as you've got your head into the late '60s, try the Card frosh who led off WITH a 16-6 record in 1967 and won only two more games after that before his wing folded. One.

**5.** Remember the Coast League star who gave the Senators a .295 season in 1950? An outfielder, his only other season of note was 1954 when he chased Avila a while for the bat crown before fading to .319. By then a Yankee, he later made several more stops before ending in 1960. One.

**6.** He won 28 games as a yearling. No one in this century has done better. That's all you should need for a single.

**7.** A later-day umpire, he's generally not remembered as having led the NL in winning percentage in 1945 while knocking off 19 victories as a Card rook. Only nine more wins were added to his column by 1949 when the Reds dumped him. Being told he was the Cards' beleaguered starter in the classic ten-homer game with the Pirates in 1947 may help you get two.

**8.** Another of those oldies but goodies, he led the NL in winning percentage his first two years on the mound. They were 1895 and 1896, and after he won 22 games in 1897 he had 78 wins in his first three seasons—all for the Orioles.

He registered only 14 more, however, before ending with Cleveland in 1901. Two.

**9.** A two-run shot for the righty who led the NL in strike-outs as a rook in 1906. He divided the season between the Cards and Cubs and was the NL leader in starts in 1909 when he went 15-21 for the Birds. Around as late as 1916 with the Indians, he sounds too easy to go so high. To which I'd agree, except I know you won't get him.

**10.** This Athletic rookie no-hit the Nats late in 1947. He came in at a cool 10-5 that year but was pretty dreary after that and was good for only five more wins. The no-hit info keeps this to a single.

**11.** Another Athletic hurler who stunned in his first full season was the port-sider who won 20 in 1949. The following year he lost 20, and that was the way it went for the remainder of his 12-year career. One.

**12.** You'll probably look up the answer to this, shake your head, murmur a curse or two at yours truly and move on—but that won't change the fact that this rook was the Reds' hill ace in 1900 while winning 17 and working in 323 innings. He leaped to the Indians for the 1901 season and that proved his undoing; he was sent away after a seven-win encore. Three-run homer.

**13.** Called "Iron Man," he showed why when he won 24 as a Phil rook in 1898 and led the NL in shutouts. A year later he won 23, but although he lasted four more seasons—all as a regular starter—he (like so many others we've met here) never matched that big frosh season. Homer.

**14.** The Red Sox for years have been famous for coming up with pitching rookies who have great yearling seasons and then are never factors again. This righty's no exception. He was 12-2 in 1969, but he won only eight more games in the five years that followed. One.

*Potential Hits: 14*
*Potential Points: 25*
*Bonus Points: 3*

*(Answers on Page 170)*

The "Iron Man" won 24 games as a rookie and led NL in shutouts. (Question 13)

# Unlikely Heroes

**1.** In the bigs since 1967 and the possessor of a lifetime average in the .250s, he put it all together in 1973 when he banged .303 for the Brewers and added 25 homers and 93 RBIs. An outfielder, he never came close to those figures again and in fact played regularly only one more year after that when he reverted to normal and hit .226. One.

**2.** This clubber did our man above even better in 1970 when he pounded 32 homers, 115 RBIs and a .315 average. Over 13 seasons as an outfielder/first-sacker, he had a .252 average when he finished in 1974 and only one other season in which he broke .270. One.

**3.** Over nine seasons as a big league regular he hit only 124 homers. One year he went as low as five; the year following, however, he struck for 43 and became only the third NL'er in history to register 40 homers and less than 100 RBIs in the same season. One.

**4.** In 1911 this Brave gardener missed the NL bat crown by a single point when he hit .333 and led the league in hits. It was only his second season and never again did he have a full season of regular play, though he continued until 1915 to be one of the game's finest pinch-hitters. Two.

**5.** This Indian looked like another Gehrig in 1930, his first full season as a regular, when he hit .349 and knocked in 136 runs. The following year he shot up to .351, but his decline after that was sudden and sharp. After a .267 season with the 1934 Red Sox, he was gone. Two.

**6.** As a part-timer in 1937 this Pale Hose flychaser showed little. But in 1938 he clubbed .331 as their regular right-fielder and looked like their next star. A year later, after falling to .171, his big league light went out forever. Homer.

**7.** In 1973 this rookie Phil outfielder stunned everyone by rapping .340 in pinch-hit roles and leading the NL with 16 pinch bingles. While playing the outfield, however, he hit only .111 and finished at .238 overall. Never more than a marginal performer in the years since. One.

**8.** Over the 12 years between 1948 and 1959 he won only 87 games. But in 1953, while toiling for the lowly Senators, he led the AL with 22 wins and nine shutouts. It was the only season he won more than 13. One.

**9.** The AL leader in mound appearances and saves in 1947 was not, believe it or not, Joe Page. It was a bespectacled Indian righty who was never much of a presence on the big league stage again. His 11-13 as a frosh in 1944 was his only other season of consequence. Two.

**10.** For most of his seven-year career he was hit hard, and even in 1965 he posted only a 3.79 ERA. However, that season he was also good for 22 wins and was the Reds' hill ace. Remember him? A bunt single says no.

**11.** Clocking an 11-8 record as a Card rook in 1955, he showed nothing for the rest of the decade. But in 1961 he led the AL in appearances and saves while coming in with a 15-5 mark. In later years he was only twice more in the win column. One.

**12.** He played with both St. Louis clubs in the middle '30s and had only one season as a regular. That came for the Browns in 1934 and he made it a good one, leading the club in RBIs with 101 and tying Pete Fox for the AL lead in double plays by an outfielder. Finished in 1936 after two years as a Brownie part-timer. Two-run homer.

**13.** A single for the NL ERA champ in 1974? Sounds like gravy, and by telling me the 16-game winner who came in at 2.28 you've got it. Needless to say, those 16 wins are about half of his big league total.

**14.** This one's tough enough for three. Over parts of eight seasons this gardener had a .295 lifetime average and only one year as a full-fledged regular. That came as a Phil in 1933 when he led the NL in at-bats and knocked 200 hits and a .309 average. I might also mention he was the runner-up to Pepper Martin for the stolen base lead.

*Potential Hits: 14*
*Potential Points: 25*
*Bonus Points: 1*

*(Answers on Page 170)*

# Minor League Magicians

*Here they are—the minor league greats who somehow never got much more than a fast shell game under the big tent. Out of kindness to you we're concentrating mostly on players from the second half of this century and omitting stars like Leo "Muscles" Shoals who tore up the lower minors but never spent a day in a big league suit. Even so, imagine how much some of these neglected aces must wish they were around now in this expansion-diluted era.*

**1.** The natural man to lead off with is the Cub outfielder who actually got in a full season of work in 1942 and swatted .300 between his years of burning up the Coast League. The NL's top pinch-hitter in 1944, he gave his last sigh of disappointment in 1946 when the Phils let him go. Just one for this Russian banger.

**2.** He holds the record for the highest lifetime average among players who were active more than ten seasons in organized baseball. His major league marks, though, show only a .192 in parts of two seasons in the '30s with the Braves and Dodgers. By then this lefty clubber was near the end of the line. Two for yet another Coast League bammer.

**3.** Managers in the Cardinal chain made hay for years when the Birds kept sending this slugging first-sacker down. Seasoning wasn't what he needed; but by the time he finally got his first real shot with the 1953 Yankees, he was 32. Still, in 70 games he hit .297 before going to the A's where he found a regular job in 1954, albeit too late for him to showcase his true talents. Two.

**4.** Rochester and Columbus fans loved the Cards and Pirates for ignoring this Triple A star all through the '50s. In 1962 the expansion Angels gave him a look, mostly at first base, though his true position was the outfield. By then 35, he only managed a .196 in 87 games, but old IL fans well remember him. Three.

**5.** Some called him Tex, others knew him as Wheels. The Tigers called him too old, though, when they finally brought him up for a look in 1953 at age 34. An outfielder, he'd burned holes through fences all across the Southwest and for years ranked among the top hitters in the upper minors. Two-run homer.

**6.** The minor league player of the year in 1950 got a very brief fling with the 1951 Browns before departing again for the farms. A rangy lefty swinger, he'd find a home today, hands down, on somebody's roster. Best known as the cat for whom Gaedel pinch-hit. That clue drops this from a probable homer to only two.

**7.** Oklahoma City fans marveled for years that the Indians could continue to bury this huge first-sacker. In his only hour with the big boys he hit .333 in a handful of games in 1950 and gave Indian fans an enormous homer that eclipsed even Easter's shots to remember. Three-run homer.

**8.** This early day Triple A phenom's problem was that no one ever decided whether he belonged on the mound or in the outfield. For the Miracle Braves he was a solid 6-2 performer and led the NL in relief wins. Ten years later the A's tested him in their pasture, then returned him to the minors where he starred for many more seasons. Four.

**9.** His minor league strikeout totals in the '40s look like misprints. Getting a shot with the Browns in 1948 after coming to them from the Indians in the Zoldak deal, he got off to a shaky start and was converted to a reliever. It wasn't his groove—although in 1952 he did manage to lead the AL in mound appearances while toiling for the White Sox. Most of his later career he spent moving between the minors, where he continued to start and star, and the majors, where managers kept hiding his lefty firepower in the bullpen. Still around with the Reds as late as 1957 when he was 36. Two.

**10.** He, Lou Ortiz and Jack Cassini were the trio of Triple A infielders in the early '50s who everyone agreed would have been good enough to play in the majors if they hadn't been too old. Cassini had had a shot with the Pirates as a pinch-runner in 1949, Ortiz never got so much as a cup of coffee, and our man finally made it up in 1956 for a month or two with the A's. In 45 games, most of them at first, though third was his home, he hit .271 before returning to the minors. If Cassini and Ortiz rang no bells, you'll be unlikely to toll this man's chimes for a two-run shot.

**11.** He got a rap while with the Braves in the late '30s for worrying more about his personal stats than about the fortunes of the team. Who could fault him, considering the caliber of most of the outfits he played on? Still, he stuck long enough to crack 77 homers—eight of them for the 1948 Pirates, his last big league stop. For years afterwards he murdered Coast League chuckers, and his name mentioned even today in LA or San Francisco often evokes more response than the names of current Dodger and Giant stars. One.

**12.** You can probably guess who's going to bring down the curtain. None other than the man who wowed Triple A fans all over the globe for nearly 20 years, from the mid-'40s to the mid-'60s, and managed to get in over 600 bigtop games in that period as well. The Pirates got his best work in 1959 and 1960. He was past 35 by then, but he still knew where the seats were and his glove work around first base made the man he alternated with look all the worse by comparison. One of those guys who could still knock 'em out today if you stuck a bat in his hands, he'd shown by the end of his career that he could have done his act in the bigs all along if only someone had been patient enough early on to stick with him through one of his notorious spring slow starts. One.

*Potential Hits: 12*
*Potential Points: 30*
*Bonus Points: 4*

*(Answers on Page 171)*

---

# 6TH INNING
# Nobody Knows My Name
# (1940-1949)

---

**1.** If it wasn't for the war, I probably never would've gotten my chance to play regularly. But one of those years that I did—1944—all I did was lead the NL in triples and stolen bases. Kiner's coming in 1946 sent me to the bench and subsequently to the Braves, where I finished the season and my career. A deuce says you don't remember the Buccos' wartime swiftie.

**2.** Beginning in 1943 I patrolled the outfield for the Red Sox until they shipped me to the Nats in 1948. I never quite got going, though in 1943 and again in 1945 I played pretty much regularly. In the 1946 Series I played in five contests and swatted a homer in the fifth game. Three.

**3.** The Phils dug my late-season debut in 1940 and gave me a regular garden post the next year. I slapped .305 in 1941 and added 18 homers. Never again did I match those figures. Passed on to the Cards in 1943, I got in two Series before going over to the Braves and missed being in my third when Boston dealt me to the Reds early in 1948. Lifetime .281, with close to 1000 hits, I'll be just about your easiest bingle this inning.

**4.** Many thought my glove was better than either Lou's or Martie's, but few talked about my bat. They all forget I led the NL in doubles in 1947, the year I also smacked 19 homers and knocked in 87 runs. Admittedly, those weren't typical figures for me, but I did amass nearly 1300 hits while covering ground for the Reds, Braves, Phils and Cards. One.

**5.** As a rook in 1940 I rapped .303 for the Browns. Two years later I shot up to .313. After the war I slipped a bit, but the Indians thought enough of my talents to trade for me in 1948 and make me their right-fielder for much of that season. But the Series wasn't my dish—I hit only .077—and after a slow start with the Pirates in 1949 I said goodbye to the bigs. Two.

**6.** I hit .305 for the Red Sox in 1945 in 100 games and .301 the following year in 61. Still, the Sox let me go to the Senators in 1947; and after two years of spot duty in their pasture, I took my .275 average in 408 games and went quietly. Homer.

**7.** For the most part I was a wartime fill-in, giving the Indians three years of duty at first base and then a few final games in 1946 before departing. I had pretty fair power, though, and in 1944 I led the AL in at-bats while rapping 13 homers off those war-dejuiced balls. Three.

**8.** I caught for the Yankees, Indians, A's and Red Sox and was a first-stringer as late as 1948 at age 34. Two years earlier I hit .283 for the A's, a figure I matched with the Indians in 1943. Even the casual '40s fans should rap me for one.

**9.** The Red Sox gave me a start in 1940, then let me pass on to the Senators two years later. For the Nats I had several fine seasons, twice hitting over .300 and leading the AL in triples in 1942. Sorry now, the Red Sox dealt for me to fill their right-field hole in 1948 and assure them the pennant, but it didn't turn out that way since I was 33 by then and had little left. The Browns got my last gasp in 1949. One.

**10.** I always wanted to play for my hometown Bengals, but such was not to be. Instead, I wound up giving the Pirates some six years of solid outfield play, most of them before the war. My best was 1940 when I hit .273 and knocked in 111 runs. After retiring, I returned to Detroit where I died in 1965. Three says you don't remember me.

**11.** The Cards, Phils and Cubs all liked the way I played the keystone sack. In my one Series after my 1944 debut I tagged a neat .412. Three years later, by now with the Phils, I had my best all-around year, hitting .285 in 155 games. Two's staked you don't know me.

**12.** The BoSox regular catcher in the 1946 Series, I went 0 for 13. In 1944, though, I hit .330, mostly with the Sox; and in 1947, after being dealt in the early going to the Tigers for Tebbetts, I had enough left to swat .273. I also caught a lot for the A's in the early '40s and finished up with their crosstown rivals in 1949. With all that info you can't miss a double, but my guess is you will.

**13.** Where's my grandslam, you're wondering about now? Okay, here I am. A Brave rookie outfielder in 1948, I got into two Series games and went hitless in four at-bats. Over the regular season I hit .277 in 90 games and went .263 the following year in 53 games. Not bad figures, but I was told to hit the road anyway. So I was a lifetime .271 hitter in 143 games and a righty all the way. If you get me, I'll cheer mighty loud, for no one's thought of—much less mentioned—my name in many moons.

**14.** Who backed up that Red Sox catcher who went 0 for 13 in the 1946 Series? Well, stop racking your brain. I'm your man, and in that same Series I went only 1 for 10. You might better remember me as the Red Sox regular mask man in 1943 and 1944. Or as the backup to Les Moss for the 1948 Browns. Worth four if you do.

*Potential Hits: 14*
*Potential Points: 33*
*Bonus Points: 3*

*(Answers on Page 171)*

---

7TH INNING
# Death in the Afternoon

**1.** Pass up this grandslam. You won't begin to recall the World War I casualty who died while in uniform after spending part of 1917 in the A's outfield. Only 23 at the time, he was being counted on by Connie but never came back.

**2.** He broke in with Washington in 1895, won 27 with the Orioles in 1898 and 19 with the Dodgers the following year. Near the close of the 1901 campaign he died while still in Dodger garb. Even knowing about those big-win years, you've still got a rugged homer.

**3.** One of baseball's classic screwballs, he died in 1912 at 30 after being jettisoned when McGraw wearied of his antics during the previous campaign. An 18-game winner for the 1909 Giants and the NL's top loser while a Card in 1908, he was done-in by demon rum. Single.

**4.** This outfielder/first-sacker was a Pirate regular and had also played full-time previously with the Giants before he succumbed to illness after the 1900 season. A good hitter, he'd led the Giants in RBIs in 1899 and was right up there among the Pirate leaders when he fell ill. Four.

**5.** The Dodgers' regular second-sacker in 1931, he was bumped off the job by Cuccinello in 1932. Moving over to the Phils in 1933, he was their regular at second through the early going but died shortly after the 4th of July. Hit .262 in four seasons. Three.

**6.** This slender Pilot rookie right-hander died at his home in Puerto Rico after the 1969 season. Only 20 at the time, he seemed to have it all ahead of him. Two-run shot, and even Pilot fans will have to dig into their memory chambers as he was only 1-3 in eight appearances.

**7.** You won't miss scoring one for this longtime Brownie and Yankee pitching ace who perished late in the 1928 season after taking his last turn on the rubber earlier in that campaign. Four times a 20-game winner for the Browns in the early '20s, he was 18-6 on the Murderers' Row outfit the year before his death shocked all.

**8.** The Phils' top hurler in the mid-'90s, he lost 29 for the Cards after moving to them in 1898 and a year later was in Redleg garb. One of the great tipplers of that era, he died prior to the 1900 season at only 26 with 120 career wins already under his belt. With those stats I can't give you more than a trey.

**9.** Another hill king whose lights went out before he was 30 was this ex-Cub, Pirate and Yankee righty who didn't live to see the start of the 1916 campaign. His first big league game was a shutout for the Cubs in 1909, and a year later he scored 20 and led the NL in winning percentage. After 18 wins in 1911, however, he fell off sharply. Two's a present.

**10.** A freak accident claimed the life of this moundsman after the 1976 season. A longtime NL relief luminary, his best years were with the Mets. One.

**11.** John died prior to the 1892 season after winning 19 for the Boston Associations a year earlier; in 1889 he'd won 22 for Cleveland—no mean feat with that bunch. William died a year later after playing left field all of 1892 (oddly replacing another earlier ill-fated Dodger star there in 1891) and putting in his sixth successive season as a big league regular. Why are these two linked together? Because though their first names differed, they both played under the same nickname and surname. It's three beside your name if you know it.

*Potential Hits: 11*
*Potential Points: 30*
*Bonus Points: 4*

*(Answers on Page 171)*

# $8$TH INNING
# One-Year Wonders

**1.** The Phils' regular second-sacker in 1944, he hit .267 in 118 games and looked more than okay, but the Phils didn't agree and he was never heard from again. Homer.

**2.** Another Phil keystoner who gave them one year of regular duty and then was pink-slipped was this Missouri boy who hit .236 in 1940. Five years later his brother played a season or so at third for the wartime Browns. Three.

**3.** His real name was Hamrick, but he played under a pseudonym for the 1890 season. Patrolling the pasture along with Farmer Weaver and Chicken Wolf, he did his share to bring the Louisville Associations the pennant by hitting .272 and scoring 93 runs. Two-run homer.

**4.** One of the most famous one-year wonders was the Phil first-sacker who clouted .324 in a 1930 debut. Five years later his brother rapped .462 for the Dodgers in a short trial. Incredibly, neither ever got a further chance. Two for either of these luckless sibs.

**5.** Okay, this switch-sticking utility man was a long way from a regular, but he narrowly missed breaking the AL rookie record for pinch-hits in 1971 when he cracked 16 for the Indians while playing in 80 games. Homer to rhyme with his nickname.

**6.** In 1902 as a 23-year-old he started 30 games for the Phils and clocked in at 11-18 with 106 strikouts. The Phils never offered him another contract despite those stats. Four.

**7.** The Association's loss leader with 24 as a 23-year-old frosh for Syracuse in 1890, he also won 17 in his 352 innings of work. But he died at 80 without ever throwing another pitch in big league competition. Grandslam.

**8.** How about another grandslam for the lefty with the St. Louis Feds who finished at 8-20 in 1914 in his only outing?

**9.** Nicknamed "Oyster Joe," he was a prominent figure in baseball circles for many years. Only one of them, however, was spent in big league mail. That came in 1924 when as a 35-year-old rook he went 6-8 in 125 innings of work for the

Nats and gave them a near-perfect inning of relief work in the Series in his last bigtop appearance. Two.

**10.** You're panting about now for a modern one-year wonder, so guess the Cub southpaw who was 4-13 in 151 innings in 1948. He possessed a gun for an arm, and his strikeout total was one of the NL's better ones in spite of those relatively few innings. Sadly, he never got another shot. Three.

**11.** The Players League-riddled Philadelphia Associations gave their shortstop job to this 19-year-old in 1890 and found no reason to keep him when he coughed up a .171 batting average and .893 glove work. Philadelphia fans quickly forgot him, and I'll go you a grandslam that you never knew enough about him to remember.

**12.** The Redlegs finished last their first season in the NL. One of the reasons was the work of this righty who divided the mound chores with Cherokee Fisher and racked up a dismal 4-26 record. Oldies experts may score a grandslam on this one, but you modern boys might just as well skip merrily ahead.

*Potential Hits: 14*
*Potential Points: 44*
*Bonus Points: 13*

*(Answers on Page 171)*

# 9TH INNING
# Switch-Hitters

*Another new wrinkle, and you'll only see it this once. So start thinking ambidextrous thoughts.*

**1.** No one doubts that you know that Mickey Mantle holds the record for homers by a switch-hitter, and you may even know that Reggie Smith is second on the list. How about a single for the third man?

**2.** He played regularly at first base for three AL clubs from 1921 through 1932 and was an excellent baserunner and the possessor of one of the most discriminating pairs of switch-hit eyes ever, compiling over 1000 career walks. Top years were with the Tigers, but the Pale Hose got a .304 season with 127 walks out of him at age 34 in 1931. Two.

**3.** Before Pete Rose came along Frankie Frisch held the record for most hits by a switch-sticker. Take two if you know who used to be second on the ambi list and is presently third. The clue that he's not in the Hall of Fame will steer you off Max Carey.

**4.** From 1965 through 1972 the Dodgers had three switch-sticks in their infield. One of course was Maury's, but the other two also showed flashes of brilliance at times, although they usually wound up somewhere around .260. For a couple of years they played side by side, and each saw Series action. You need both to score an easy bingle.

**5.** He played first base for eight different clubs between 1895 and 1908. The Giants received most of his best days, but the Cards, Orioles and Washington Nationals got some good mileage out of him too. Big, he could hit hard and long from both sides of the plate. In 1905, his only Series season, he hit .299, rapped five homers and swiped 22 sacks—a representative year in all ways. Three.

**6.** Nicknamed "Union Man," this first-sacker moved from the Giants to the Braves in 1919 and then was dealt to the Phils in 1923. Had his two finest seasons with them before wrapping it up with the Reds in 1925. A notorious first-ball hitter. Four.

**7.** The Gas House gang had another switch-stick besides Frisch's. This stroker led the NL in homers and slugging in 1934 and was still a dangerous clubber as late as 1938 when he formed part of the nucleus of another NL pennant winner. One.

**8.** And still a third Gas House switch-clouter was their right-fielder in the middle '30s who bounced back for two fine seasons after seeming finished following a .196 season in 1932 divided between the Red Sox and the White Sox. Top average came in 1929 when he hit an even .300 for the Crimson Hose, though with the 1934 Cards he led the NL in at-bats and scored 106 runs. One.

**9.** The Association batting leader with Baltimore in 1889, he switched to the Braves the following year and compiled nearly 1900 hits before hanging 'em up after spending the 1899 season with the Spiders. One of the game's top first-

This switch hitter and switch pitcher played every position except catcher. (Question 14)

sackers in the last century, he wasn't too many notches behind Brouthers and Anson. Two.

**10.** Another star of the 1890s was this Cub gardener who led the NL in homers in 1890 and four years later had his top all-around season when he hit .330 and knocked in 130 runs. A real oddity for his time in that he played all ten of his seasons in the same league and never played so much as a single inning anywhere but in the outfield. Four.

**11.** One of the game's top switch-sticks at the moment belongs to this AL flychaser who's currently with his third bigtop club. In the NL in 1973 he hit .302 and rapped 23 homers and 103 RBIs, but he bettered all but one of those figures in 1977. One.

**12.** Another modern switcher is this shortstop whose bat remains his Achilles heel, though he's always among the NL leaders in triples. One.

**13.** The Pirates passed this switch-stick on to the Braves for the 1948 season. Illness kept him out of the Series that year, and he never really got his eye back. With the Pirates, though, he had five solid seasons, including a high of .312 in 1944. Three.

**14.** This switch-hitter was also a switch-thrower. On the mound, mostly for Association clubs, he won 285 games. As a batsman he rapped only .243 but at times played every position except catcher. Oldie fans will nail a bingle cold.

*Potential Hits: 14*
*Potential Points: 27*
*Bonus Points: 0*

*(Answers on Page 171)*

**Game**

**6**

# Nobody Knows My Name
# (1950-1959)

**1.** The Brownies got a full year out of me at second in 1950 before Uncle Sam took me away. Dealt to the Tigers upon my return in 1953, I split that year between them and the Indians in utility roles. Sent down for a time, I returned with the 1955 Red Sox, got in a few weeks' work with them and then a few more with the Cubs before leaving for good. If it weren't for Uncle Sam, though, Bobby Young might never have gotten the Browns' keystone job away from me because as a rook I hit eight homers and knocked in 50 runs, figures Bobby never came close to matching. Three.

**2.** The White Sox couldn't find room for me and sent me to the A's in 1954. The A's regular centerfielder that season, I split the job in 1955 with another nobody you'll meet later on. Power was my game—32 homers over two seasons—but my .222 average hurt. Homer.

**3.** After several years in the Indian's chain, I was shuffled on to the Browns where I found a home at third in 1951 and rapped .243 in 130 games. It was my only full season as a regular, although in 1955 I batted over 300 times for the Orioles in utility roles. By then I'd also played for the White Sox and Nats. I'm tough, but the two ahead of me were tougher, so just two.

**4.** Well, in case you were beginning to wonder whether you knew anything at all about the '50s, here I am to reassure you. Twice a bona fide .300 hitter as the Orioles' regular first-sacker, I carried a .293 average over nine seasons. The Pale Hose saw me first, the Braves last. One.

**5.** I played a bit in the late '40s with the Pale Hose and the Yankees, but it wasn't until I came to the Browns in 1950 that I started to work steady in the AL. For the next five-and-a-half seasons I was pretty much a fly-chasing regular, mostly with the Tigers who caged me in 1952. Top year was 1953 when I went .288 with 11 homers. Don't say I'm Don Lund. Don was okay, but I was a lot more than that in my over-800 bigtop games. One.

**6.** No self-respecting '50s fan should miss singling on me. I was the Red Sox first-sacker before and after Harry A. and rapped over 100 homers wearing crimson socks before moving on to the Cubs in 1960. Peak output was 1956 when I hit .291 in 106 games. Part of the Red Sox baby movement in 1952, I was one of the few who stuck.

**7.** As the Browns' first-sacker in 1950 I clubbed 22 homers. Three years later, back with the Browns after stints with the White Sox, Red Sox and Tigers, I rapped .317 in 97 games while playing mostly left field. In 1954 I drifted off to the minors. I was never one of your modern Ty Cobbs on the bases, but I could hit a wicked ball. And of the four clubs I played with only the Tigers didn't get their money's worth. Never could hit in Briggs. Two.

**8.** You've already heard from the cat who split the A's center garden with me in 1955. Next to him I was Speaker; in 1955 I hit an even .300 and the following two years I led the AL in triples. As far back as 1952 I was the Indians' right-fielder after burning up the Coast League. On occasion I played first, too, and I once knocked in 105 runs. In my only Series in 1957 I hit only .083, but the club I was with didn't use me enough to keep me sharp. One.

**9.** Your grandslammer this inning, I was a nine-game winner for the Indians in 1953—9-3 in 112 innings, in fact—and I wielded a mean stick besides. For the record-setting 1954 champs I got into 14 games before being cut loose. Telling you I was one of the first black hurlers in the bigs is your gift from me.

**10.** The Giants kept thinking I was going to break through big, and frankly so did I. In 1951 I was 5-1; a year later that was upped to 6-1; and in 1953, my year of greatest toil, I went 6-4 in 106 innings. I won only one game after that, however, and after 1955 they all gave up on me. But Leo hasn't forgotten all those springs he thought sure I'd become a Polo Grounds fixture. No, please don't say Roger Bowman. Two.

**11.** The Phils liked me enough after my rookie outing in 1950 to make me a part of their one-two punch with Robin in 1951. I won 15 for them that year; but after shifting over to the Reds early in 1952, I lost my smoke and even the putrid Cubs wouldn't keep my dead wing around past the first days of the 1955 season. Yeah, I was a southern boy and my nickname shows it. One.

**12.** Red Sox fans score an easy one here; the rest of you may have to run it out. You really shouldn't, though, because over the last six years of the '50s I won 78 games in Yawkey garb, including 19 in 1956. My hose went in 1961 when I was only 30, but by then I'd had eight seasons. And, hey, I could hit that apple too.

**13.** Tall, handsome, the possessor of a smooth lefty stroke, I got lengthy looks from the Dodgers, Cubs, Pirates, Indians and A's. In 1958 I hit .284 in 129 games after going to KC in the Power deal. That was my pinnacle, but as far back as 1948 Leo thought enough of me to pencil my name in ahead of Hodges for a time. One.

**14.** You should be batting 1.000 this inning, so I'll try to bring you down to earth a little. In 1951 I shared the Reds' left-field post with Adcock after playing regularly there for most of the previous year. I was a long while making it back upstairs; it was another six years, in fact, before I handled the Senators' centerfield slot for a season. So, three years of pretty much steady duty in the '50s and a long trial with the Reds in 1946. I could go get 'em—nobody ever gave me anything but praise for my glove—but at the dish I was only .235 lifetime. One of the least-remembered gardeners of the '50s, I'm going for a homer in 1978.

*Potential Hits: 14*
*Potential Points: 28*
*Bonus Points: 3*

*(Answers on Page 171)*

# 2ND INNING
# It's All Relative

**1.** Jiggs played the infield and Tacky Tom the outfield, and for a few weeks in 1893 they were teammates on the Cubs. Tom moved over to the Reds later that season then subsequently to the Cards where he finished in 1896 with a .301 average lifetime. Jiggs had some lung trouble and died three years after leaving the game in 1895. The surname of these sibs will bring three.

**2.** At age 43 Johnny caught his brother for the 1948 Pirates. Johnny never did much in the bigs, playing only 98 games over parts of seven seasons, but his younger brother had spells of being one of the NL's top righties. One.

**3.** These two sibs were teammates for an AL team throughout the '20s. One's in the Hall of Fame and the other caught over 1500 games in the bigs and piloted another 1260. Enough there for a bingle.

**4.** The 1911 Cards had a brother act on the mound. The younger sib, a lefty, was by far the more effective for them, but a year later he faded while his righty brother went on to pitch for the Browns, Tigers, Indians and White Sox. Finishing at 5-5 with the Black Sox crew, he'd gone 13-18 while splitting 1915 between the Browns and Bengals. Four.

**5.** Teammates in the early '20s with the Giants, both were righties and both also pitched, at different times, for the Braves. There the similarities about end, for the older sib was one of the NL's best for years, leading the league with 25 wins in 1919 and winning 153 lifetime. The younger boy wasn't bad—61 wins total and 16 in 1924—but he was definitely the lesser of the two. One.

**6.** A rugged pair to remember. Fred gave the Braves a year as a utility man before hopping to the Feds for two years of regular action—1914 at third for Buffalo and 1915 at short for Brooklyn. The Cards had him last for a short stretch in 1917. Charlie, who was 11 years older, broke in for the sibs' hometown Cleveland outfit in 1902 but had his best days later with the Nats, Red Sox and Cubs. The NL's top bullpen winner in 1912, he scored 12 as a Red Sox starter two years earlier and twice worked over 200 innings for the Nats. Take a two-run shot for their surname.

**7.** And speaking of brothers who had a big age difference, how about this pair of righties who celebrated their big league debuts 30 years apart? Older brother Jesse was 1-1 in 13 games for the 1924 Cards and was soon forgotten, but his kid sib had a 12-10 frosh season for another NL club in 1954 and was an effective Angel reliever well into the '60s. Also with the 1959 NL champs, he and Jesse easily hold the sib record for the greatest difference between their years as active performers. One.

**8.** Joe rapped .423 for the 1894 Cards in seven games, then was dropped, despite the complaints of his brother who was the Cards' regular backstopper. Joe's brother went on to catch later for the Reds and Pirates and for over a decade was one of the NL's premier receivers. A good hitter, he never hooked on with a pennant winner, and that's why he's not much better remembered today than Joe. Three.

**9.** The people in Veto, Alabama, have never forgotten these two righty brothers, though most others will be hard put to double here. The elder Veto boy was a Brownie mainstay for several years before switching over to the Giants in 1936 and becoming one of the NL's top firemen in the late '30s. The younger lad also chucked for the Browns, but not till 1940 by which time he'd put in three very mediocre years in the Tigers' bullpen.

**10.** Which four of the following Hall of Famers had neither fathers, sons nor brothers who also played in the majors? Ty Cobb, Honus Wagner, Jim O'Rourke, George Kelly, Eddie Collins, Ray Schalk, Buck Ewing, Rube Marquard, John Clarkson, Johnnie Evers, Hank Aaron, Heinie Manush, Christy Mathewson and Zack Wheat? (Okay, Aaron's not in there yet, but anybody wanna bet against his making it?) One base for each right guess; one base subtracted for each wrong guess.

**11.** As a Red Sox utility infielder in 1929 and 1930 he was no great shakes, but he fathered a son who was one of the AL's top firemen two-and-a-half decades later. The kid did pop proud in 1955, in fact, when he went 8-1 in the bullpen with 19 saves and won his only start for an overall 9-1 while leading the AL in both saves and appearances. You won't need the son's team to score one.

**12.** Jack went 7-5 in 113 innings for the 1911 Tigers in his only big league juncture. Thirty-six years later Jack's kid had the first of his three seasons on the Reds' mound. Twice the big redhead worked in over 100 innings, but his overall 8-13 record wasn't much better than pop's. Three for this combo.

**13.** Snake was one of the AL's top lefties for the A's and Orioles in 1901 and 1902, but he was gone by the time his kid brother came on the scene with the 1904 Giants. For over a decade the kid was one of the NL's top lefties, twice winning 20 and also giving McGraw's men some sharp bullpen work. Both these sibs could hit too, Snake so well that he should have been able to catch on at another position when his arm went. Two.

**14.** While his older brother was putting together an 8-9 record for the 1928 Indians, Russ was in the throes of a dreadful 0-12 campaign for the Phils. It was Russ's last look at big league sticks, but the elder half of this sib tandem was only at the midpoint of his AL career which saw him win in double figures three times for the Indians and finish with the 1933 White Sox. Three.

*Potential Hits: 14*
*Potential Points: 34*
*Bonus Points: 1*

*(Answers on Page 172)*

3RD INNING
# Outstanding Offenders

**1.** The only NL star to hit over .380 twice and not win a batting title on either occasion did it two years in a row. A bingle.

**2.** Single again by naming the AL star who went over .390 two years in a row without winning a batting title.

**3.** A medium-tough bingle goes up on the board for the identity of the owner of the highest lifetime average by a switch-hitter in over 1000 games.

**4.** His final years were so mediocre that his AL seasons between 1947 and 1950, when he averaged nearly .310 for that period and twice knocked in over 100 runs, are forgotten. His debut was 1946 and 1956 his coda tune. The Red Sox, Indians, Giants and Orioles all had lockers with his name on them for a time, but it was as a gardener in the stadium with the red dirt track in front of the outfield wall that he made his mark. One.

**5.** The record for most hits by a player who performed in only one big league game is held by a Brownie third-sacker who went 4 for 5 in a one-day outing in 1910. Offering a grandslam may whet your appetite, but you'll only wind up with an ulcer if you think about this one too long.

In his only big league game this Brownie went
four for five. (Question 5)

**6.** He had only one season in which he batted more than 400 times, that in 1970. Yet he's slapped over 1100 career hits, averaged .303 and is one of only five men in history who've collected over 100 pinch-hits. Present-dayers will cream this for a single.

**7.** Between 1942 and 1970 only Stan Musial registered 3000 hits. For one, what player who retired in that period came the closest to becoming a second 3000-hit man?

**8.** Among the top 15 pinch-swingers are such great hitters as Enos Slaughter, Fatty Fothergill and Smokey Burgess and such pinch-strokers deluxe as Dave Philley, Gates Brown, Elmer Valo and Jerry Lynch. But there's also a modern-day NL utility man who had only one season of regular play—that for the 1964 Cubs when he split the season between short and second—and nary a season in which he hit even remotely close to .300. Yet, despite a .237 lifetime average, he somehow hung on for ten seasons and became in time one of the game's more reliable pinch-hitters. A switch-stroker, he went 0 for 2 for the Reds in Series action. Could be a difficult single.

**9.** Only one man has rapped 3000 hits on less than a .300 career average. Can't believe anyone serious about the game won't single on this one.

**10.** Who's the only swatter since 1937 to hit .350 or better three years in a row? One.

**11.** Another one for the cat who did it last in 1935-37.

**12.** Forget the first five years of the century when players jumped like jacks between the two leagues and also the years since inter-league trading became legit, and tell me the only two men between 1905 and 1960 who had seasons in each league where they appeared among the top five hitters. One had five such seasons in the AL and one in the NL and the other had three NL seasons and one in the AL. Each alone is worth a bingle, but do yourself proud and homer by getting both.

**13.** Now tell me for a double who was the only 19th-century star to win bat crowns in both the NL and the American Association.

**14.** Disregard the old National Association for this one and score three by naming the only other 19th-century player to win bat crowns in two different leagues.

# 4TH INNING
# Odds and Ends

1. In 1955 the Orioles tested a minor league second-sacker in 40 games and then let him go after a .114 showing. Six years later the Pirates brought up a catcher from their Columbus farm whom they kept around for parts of two seasons before sending on to the Nats for two more. Both these men batted left and threw right, both were almost career-long minor leaguers, and one more thing they shared—their last names were the same, and it's uncommon enough that no one else in big league history ever played under it. Oh, one more thing about them. They had the same first name too, and many fans still probably believe, in fact, that they were the same player. Two.

2. Another name's-the-same combo were these two outfielders. One had his finest hour for the 1893 Pirates when he hit .346 and knocked in 103 runs; the other's best marks were with the 1920 Indians when he too knocked in 103 runs and hit .316. That's enough for two more.

3. Want still one more name's-the-samer? Try the Brownie third-sacker who hit .306 in 103 games in 1920 and the Giant catcher who stroked .294 in 91 games that same season. It was the Brownie's last outing of note, but the Giant starred for another decade, though for a different NL team. Two.

4. How about the Cardinal catcher and left-fielder in 1952 who shared the same last name and who many fans erroneously assumed were brothers? The outfielder hit .288 in 98 games that year and went .310 for the 1953 Pirates. The catcher was good for .259 in 147 games in 1952 and was around as late as 1961 with the Angels. One.

5. These two pitching brothers played under the same first name, though one was actually named Francis and the

other Edward. Needless to say, their playing name was neither Francis nor Edward, and the only way fans of their era could keep them straight was by calling one "Big" and the other "Little." The little guy actually stood 6'3" and was an NL star for a decade, twice winning more than 20 for the Dodgers in the teens. The big man's height is unknown, and his best hour was a 13-22 for the 1906 Braves. Two for their name.

**6.** Now how about these two NL hurlers, each of whom had big years for the Cards and Phils? The elder broke in with the 1922 Tigers, moved to the NL with the Cards in 1926 and finished with the 1940 Phils. The younger came up with the 1928 Reds, moved on to the Cards in 1936 and finished with the Braves in 1947. Both won over 100 games, worked over 2000 innings, were right-handed, stood 5'11½"—and naturally had the same last name. And their first names were so similar fans of that era never were sure who was who. One.

**7.** These two outfielders could easily have appeared in other categories, but I've been saving them. Hub came up in 1910 with the Browns and went out with a bang, rapping .282 in 118 games for the 1912 Dodgers. Denny started fast as a rook by hitting .285 in 141 games for the 1928 Phils— his only full season as a regular. Then, early in 1931, Denny also wound up with the Dodgers. Their last names weren't the same, but each was only one letter away from being an adjective depicting one of the four directions. If this sounds too esoteric, move on. Should you be intrigued, just spell both their last names correctly and earn a cheap four.

**8.** After his first four seasons this gardener had a .274 average in 432 games. He finished 13 years later with a .342 career average, and would have ranked third on the all-time batting list only a few tenths of a point behind Hornsby were it not for his slow start. One.

**9.** He had only one season as a regular, that in 1966 when he hit only .243 in 120 games. Yet Cub fans won't have forgotten him, for in that one outing he set the all-time Bruin strikeout record by fanning 143 times in only 419 at-bats. Two.

**10.** One of the oddest careers among modern players is that of this former catcher/outfielder who hit .281 with 13 homers as a Card rook in 1958, then was shuffled off to the farm for most of the next two seasons before returning to rap .280 with 18 homers for the expansion Nats in 1961. A year later he again hit .280 as an Indian part-timer and clubbed 11 homers in only 143 at-bats. A few months into 1963 he was released by the Reds. It puzzled fans a generation ago why this big guy got such a short shrift, and no one in the years since has provided a good explanation. Just another, it seems, who didn't get the breaks his talented bat should have brought him. Two.

**11.** Two who got all the breaks are these ex-AL outfielders, both of whom first appeared in 1966 and carried sub-.240 batting averages into the NL in the early '70s. One, a lefty swinger, suddenly popped .295 for an NL club in 1974 after hitting .188 and .107 the previous two years in the AL. His counterpart, a righty, banged .288 in 1973 for the same NL team after going as low as .171 in 88 games for the 1969 Yankees. They were both really soaring in 1976 when the lefty hit .318 and the righty .303. With different NL clubs by then, they were both past 30 and still causing AL fans (who remembered them as busts) to shake their heads. Your clues are that the righty came to the Yanks for Clete Boyer and the lefty broke in as a switch-hitter with the Angels. Know both and get one.

**12.** Traded by the Dodgers to the Phils early in 1947, he thus missed out on becoming the first ever to play on a pennant winner and an NBA championship club. His NBA experience came after his baseball days were over. A backup center to Mikan, he'd had six big league seasons by then, two as a regular first-sacker. Top year was 1944 when he knocked in 83 runs. One of the few World War II performers who was a service reject because of his height. Easy deuce for the all-around sports fan.

**13.** Babe Ruth, Ty Cobb, Rogers Hornsby, Stan Musial, Paul Waner, Ted Williams and Jimmy Foxx all made more than 60 pinch-hit appearances during their careers. Only one of them averaged .300 as a pincher, however, and that by just a couple of points. What's it prove? You decide. I've decided it's only worth one.

**14.** Here's a real mind-blower that you'll need a pencil and paper for. Three of the top five first-sackers on the total games played at that position list are not in the Hall of

Fame; the same is true for two of the top five second-sackers, three of the top five shortstops and no less than *four* of the top five third-basemen. Twelve names here; ten right in twelve guesses earns four, three for nine right, two for eight, single for seven, zip for less.

*Potential Hits: 14*
*Potential Points: 27*
*Bonus Points: 0*

*(Answers on Page 172)*

---

5TH INNING
# The Ignoble and the Ignominious

*You won't believe I've dug up still more bad guys for you after some of the jewels I stuck you with in the last book. And it's true I've had to scramble a bit here. Only enough to fill out this one inning. But each is worth at least a full carat. Step right up to the counter and make your own appraisal.*

**1.** How this guy's managed to hang on for over a decade is a puzzle indeed. Since 1966 he's patrolled the outfield in the bigs for at least part of every season but has never once played regularly; he's displayed only so-so power, has a lifetime average under .230 and a penchant for striking out. The White Sox especially seem enamored of him, holding a place for him on their roster for all or part of nine of the last 12 seasons. His only year of consequence was 1969 when he rapped .256 in 93 games and added 11 homers. One.

**2.** Another who lasted long and showed little was this gardener who broke in with the A's in 1963 and finally convinced everyone he didn't belong after a .200 season in 1972 with the Brewers. In the years between he once batted over 300 times in a season for the A's and knocked in only 20 runs, this after a .206 effort in 101 games for the 1967 Mets. Well, he probably had power, you say, or maybe he could run. Try 12 stolen bases and a like amount of homers in over 500 games. And a .226 average. In a shortstop maybe that kind of output could be accepted, but an outfielder? Two.

**3.** And about those shortstops. The all-time worst lifetime average among players in over 1000 games belongs to this former Phil and Expo who broke in like a champ with a .244 effort in 1962. A champ anyway considering he broke .230 only once after that, as a regular in 1971 when he got into 159 games for the Expos. Back trouble hurt him, but his stick cost him more, for his glove was among the absolute best at short. If he only could've reversed the last two digits of his .215 lifetime average, he would easily have been an All-Star many times over. One.

**4.** Those low-average men intrigue. The poorest single season performance ever by a man in over 180 at-bats was turned in by the rookie Brave shortstop who rattled NL hurlers for a .122 average in 1912. It took him nine seasons to live that down so that someone would give him a regular job. The Senators eventually did in 1921, and he went on to play steadily over the next decade at second, short and third for a variety of AL teams—mainly the Browns. And lo! when he finished, his lifetime average was up to .254. Four.

**5.** A couple more in the same vein. Who's the only man ever to compile over 2800 hits on less than a .270 lifetime average? One.

**6.** What about this minor league star who holds the major league record for the worst lifetime average among players who made more than 70 plate appearances? It's .097, spread out among the Giants, Reds and Indians in the '40s. Skeeter Shelton, move over; this outfielder/first-sacker belongs in your company. Grandslam.

**7.** How about the man who has the lowest lifetime average—to wit, .256—among players who've garnered more than 2000 hits? No, not the Rabbit; this man's nickname is almost a perfect antithesis, in fact. One.

**8.** Breaking your concentration, I'll now ask who the Phillie first-sacker was who was kicked out of the game as part of Landis's purge after the 1920 season. He hit .288 that year and previously had put in several seasons of regular duty for the Cards. His name's not exactly a household word—not even in my house—so I'll give a two-run homer.

**9.** Another blackballed swatter was this early NL star who led in homers and RBIs for Boston in 1879, then was told to take a walk after the following season. He hiked for three years till the Association formed, but when it did he came back to star several years for Cinci. Born Benjamin Rippay, he might be better remembered today if he'd played under that name. Homer.

**10.** Now the chuckers. In 1930 this Phil righty led the NL in mound appearances while registering an unbelievably awful 7.67 ERA. To show he meant business he came back with a 9.55 showing in 1931 and mercifully finished his four-year career with a (for him) creditable 5.77 job in 1932. He was 6.97 in over 320 innings, the worst showing ever among hurlers who labored that often. Two-run homer.

**11.** This Brownie righty gave our Phil a close battle before finishing in 1939 with a 6.74 ERA in 462 innings. His most amazing year was 1937 when he clocked in at 7.36, yet managed to complete six games and rack up the Browns' best record—9-12. Overall he was 16-38 and once, in 1935, actually pitched a shutout. Four.

**12.** In 1906 the top relief stats in the NL belonged to a Giant rook who registered six saves in 21 bullpen outings and threw a shutout in his first major league start. Big things were expected of him, but with the Braves in 1909 he suffered through the second most ignominious season by a hurler in this century when he went 5-25. Three of those five wins, granted, were shutouts. Three-run homer.

**13.** Credit for the absolutely most ignominious season ever by a 25-game loser goes, oddly enough, to another Brave who in 1935 finished at 4-25. Incredibly, only two years before that he led the NL in winning percentage while racking up 20 victories for those same Braves. Two's your prize here.

**14.** Among players who got into more than 800 games, only one holds a lifetime batting average over .250 and a slugging average under .300. A Pale Hoser most of his career, he moved to the Nats in 1952 and later to the Red Sox. A Brownie as far back as 1944, he saw most of his action at third, batted left-handed and in 1949 hit his only homer—an inside-the-park job, naturally. The question doesn't quite finish here, for in the '40s the White Sox had another regular who in over 1000 games hit .249 and had a slugging average only 34 points better. At times these two powder puffs followed each other at the tail end of the Pale Hose batting order, and one can almost imagine AL hurlers looking past them to the ever-dangerous Sox hurler in the ninth slot—say Bill Wight who one year went 0 for 61.

Anybody wonder why the White Sox brought up the rear in the late '40s? For three, name both powerless wonders. A single if you know just one.

*Potential Hits: 14*
*Potential Points: 40*
*Bonus Points: 7*

*(Answers on Page 172)*

---

# 6TH INNING
## Hose

**1.** Rap a bingle by telling me the only Cy Young winner whose career winning percentage is under .500.

**2.** A rook in 1905, this Dodger unfortunate lost 98 games in his first five seasons and won only 46 times before moving to the Cubs in 1910. Once he got some breathing space he posted a winning record from then on, but by then it was already too late to salvage his career. He finished with a .378 winning percentage. Four.

**3.** Six 30-game winners in this century had seasons in which they suffered 20 losses. Only one of them, however, lost 20 in the *same* season that he won 30. For one, who was he?

**4.** This right-hander once won 21 games for a cellar dweller. Remarkable enough right there. But incredibly he did it in 1918 while pitching for a team that played only 128 games in that war-abbreviated season! Amazing as this feat is, it's gone for the most part totally unnoticed. Four says you haven't picked up on it either.

**5.** Known as "The Curveless Wonder," he more than got by on his fastball for years. A 20-game winner with the Phils in 1901, he rang up 27 five years later with the Highlanders. Never on a pennant winner, he broke in with the Phils in 1895, and his bat was so good he frequently played the outfield on his days off. Tough two for this 185-game winner.

**6.** You all know Pappas is the only 200-game winner never to have a 20-victory season. For a bingle, tell me the only 200-game winner who never worked more than 261 innings in a season.

**7.** And another bingle comes for knowing the only 200-game winner who completed fewer than 125 games—just 109, to be exact.

**8.** Take one for the name of the NL reliever who posted a 1.03 ERA as a rook in 1974 and kayoed the soph jinx by winning 15 in 1975. As a junior, however, he was only 4-9.

**9.** Among 20th-century lefties who registered at least 120 career decisions, his .671 winning percentage is a close second to Whitey Ford's .690. The clue that he stands alone in a lot of other categories makes this rate only one.

**10.** The above southpaw had permanently immortalized this next port-sider a couple of years before they became teammates in 1929. In that 1929 campaign our man here put together a nifty 12-0 record. A perfect 3-0 in Series work, he won 185 games lifetime. Despite all this, though, he still finished in 1936 with a lifetime losing record. One.

**11.** As a Brave rook in 1942 he led the NL in relief losses. Twelve years later he led the AL in saves. The years between are the ones you'll best remember him for, however, and they weren't for his bullpen work. On flag winners in both leagues. One.

**12.** One of the classic buried careers belongs to this righty who arrived at 29 with the 1903 Pirates. Shuttled to the Braves in 1904, he lost 22 games in each of the next two seasons and in 1905 managed only four wins to go with all those defeats. The Braves said good-bye, and he disappeared till 1908 when the Dodgers—the great catch-alls for weirdo pitchers in those years—brought him back and saw him lose 21 more despite a fantastic 1.87 ERA. He was still hanging in there as late as 1921 when he came out of the bullpen four times at age 47 for the Phils while acting as their manager. His name was a bizarre as his accomplishments, and from your lips it'll bring three.

**13.** A homer awaits anyone who knows the Athletic lefty who led the AL in ERA with a grand 1.37 in 1909 while winning 18 and chalking up seven whitewashes. He was all through three years later at 25. Even Connie, if alive today, would have to think a bit before coming out with his name.

**14.** The lid shuts this inning on true expert turf. Five hurlers in this century worked more than 300 innings in their final big league seasons. Four we met in that other great book of mine, but it's still worth a single to you if you remember as many as three of them. For the fifth man, the lefty who split the 1901 season between Milwaukee and Cleveland before dropping precipitously from view after leading the AL in losses, I'll give four. Five points are possible here, so ponder a while on this one.

*Potential Hits: 14*
*Potential Points: 30*
*Bonus Points: 0*

*(Answers on Page 173)*

# 7TH INNING
# Monickers

*A few singles thrown in here for a change of pace, but most of the going this inning is definitely on the A-one expert level.*

1. Ding-a-Ling. Four.
2. Snitz. Three-run homer.
3. What's the Use. Three-run homer.
4. Motormouth. One.
5. Happy Rabbit. (You '40s fans will remember this nickname, though it's since been forgotten.) Three.
6. Ebba. One.
7. Skyrocket. Grandslam.
8. Pebbly Jack. Two.
9. Yam. Grandslam.
10. Bow Wow. One.
11. Sleeper. Grandslam.
12. Ninety-Six. One.
13. Mysterious. Grandslam.
14. Hobe. Two.
15. Spittin' Bill. One.

*Potential Hits: 15*
*Potential Points: 40*
*Bonus Points: 16*

*(Answers on Page 173)*

# Jack of All Trades

**1.** He won 20 or better several times with the Brooklyn entries in both the Association and the NL. As late as 1895 he was still tough enough to win 21 with the Cubs. A 197-game winner overall, he also played regularly at times in the outfield and twice knocked over 100 hits. If around now, his looks and general prima donna veneer would make him a hot item, but his legend over the years has grown so cold that you'll snag three for him.

**2.** Another old NL'er whose star has so dimmed over the years that not a single biographical fact is known about him today is this ex-Giant, Louisville, Brave and Washington jack of the '90s who played the outfield, all four infield positions and even pitched on occasion. A steady .280 hitter, he was the Giants' second-sacker in 1894 and the Louisville shortstop two years later, but the outfield was his favorite spot. Three-run homer.

**3.** This early day star once threw a perfect game, and in 1879 he racked up 47 wins for Providence. Ten years later he hit .369 as the Giants' shortstop. The only man ever to register more than 150 mound victories and 2000 career hits, he had to wait, incredibly, until 1964 to make the Hall of Fame. One.

**4.** A regular at times at third, short and the outfield, he also played 155 games at second. The Nats of Walter's era got his best years and the Yankees got his last in 1925. The AL leader in triples in 1921, he also hit .302 that year, but he was usually somewhere in the .250s. Two for this veteran jack of 14 bigtop seasons.

**5.** A shortstop for Milwaukee in 1901 and also for Pittsburgh in 1902, he was switched to third when he moved to the Highlanders in 1903 and also saw regular duty later in the outfield. One of the AL's top threats on the bases in its first decade, he finished with the Senators. A first-stringer in each of his 11 seasons, he never had a year in which he didn't play at least two positions. Three.

**6.** A regular at third for the 1903 Tigers and again for the Highlanders in 1905 and the Browns in 1907, he also saw frequent action at short and second. Nothing unusual

The only man with more than 150 mound victories and 2,000 hits, he waited over half a century to make the Hall of Fame. (Question 3)

there, but Dodger fans will remember him as the rookie righty who went 12-22 in 1898. Later a Tiger mound mainstay for several seasons before he won the third-base slot. Two-run homer.

**7.** Surfacing with the 1895 Cubs, he finished three years later at only 23 with a .312 lifetime average and a 23-18 record on the mound, including a 13-10 finale in 1898. He played the outfield when not on the rubber and is challenging enough, despite his fine stats, to bring you a grandslam.

**8.** The Braves had him at short for several years in the mid-'20s, then moved him to the mound where his weak bat strangely started to catch fire. He won in double figures five years in a row for the Braves and followed up with a 15-12 season, his best, after switching to the Cubs in 1932. Later gave the Braves several more steady mound seasons. A long career, but three's the ante that you've forgotten.

**9.** Still around today, he broke in at 18 as an Angel backstopper in 1962 but has since seen regular service at first and in the outfield. An all-around handyman and a good pinch-swinger, he had several seasons as a full-timer with the Royals but inconsistent bat work has relegated him mostly to utility roles. One.

**10.** His true surname was the same as that of a star halfback for the Lions in the '50s, but this switch-hitter played under a handle that matched that of an NL bat crown winner of his time. An outfielder with the Cards, he was installed at second for the Brooklyn Feds after jumping to them in 1915 and later played on and off at various positions for the Yankees, Browns, Reds, Cubs and Dodgers. All that skipping around had a reason, for he was one of the game's shady characters and was expelled by Landis. Oddly enough, so was his batting-leader namesake. Just one with all these clues.

**11.** What postwar AL star won two batting titles while playing at different infield positions after coming up as a regular at still a third infield slot? One.

**12.** Tough but fair is this next poser. The NL's top pinch-stick in his final season in 1945, he batted .301 overall in 114 games for the Phils. Fourteen of those games were spent on the mound where he'd posted a 2-6 record for the Nats in 100 innings as far back as 1940. An outfielder when not on the rubber, he died recently in Florida after fleeing his native Cuba. Three.

**13.** One of the very few catchers in modern times who also played an effective shortstop, he saw action as well at second, third and the outfield. An anemic stick held him back a bit, but he did regular plate duty for both the Astros and Expos after a fine .288 rookie season for the 1963 Pirates. One.

**14.** He posted 16-16 in his opening bow for the 1901 Senators. After a shaky mound start in 1902, the Nats made him their regular right-fielder, shuttled him between the mound and the garden in 1903 and then sent him on to Pittsburgh. There, he operated exclusively on the rubber in 1904, although he did pinch-hit effectively on occasion. One of only a handful of men in this century to win in double figures one season and rack up 100 base hits in the next, he'll cause you hours of sweat to no avail, for even knowing you're up for a grandslam won't help you score here.

*Potential Hits: 14*
*Potential Points: 35*
*Bonus Points: 9*

*(Answers on Page 173)*

# 9TH INNING
# The Unrewarded

**1.** Although he was never a league leader in a single offensive category, his name is on the 2000-hit list. Only once, in 1970, did he hit .300 as a regular, and only in 1963 did he make more than 165 hits in a season. Steady was his name and second base was his game. A crack pinch-hitter in his later years. One.

**2.** Guaranteed you'll look up this guy, murmur "Who...?" and move on. For Silent John arrived on the scene in 1903 with absolutely no fanfare and departed a decade later as quietly as he'd come. Yet for years he gave the Phils outstanding right-field play, and when he moved to the Braves in 1912 he had enough left to rap .309 that season and .297 in his finale a year later. Three.

**3.** His last at-bat came as a pinch-hitter for the Yankees in the 1925 Series. It was his only fall appearance, though for years he was one of the AL's top hitters, leading at various times in total hits, doubles, triples and RBIs (three times) while gardening alongside the greatest player of his era. Over 2000 hits and 1000 RBIs. One.

**4.** About as tough a moundsman as there was in the NL in the '20s and early '30s, he was both a starter and a reliever for the Cubs. A real scrapper, he won 20 in 1933 only, but was good for 176 victories overall. Last seen with the Reds in 1945 at age 44. One.

**5.** The Cubs passed him on to the Dodgers in 1913 after he'd given them eight top-flight seasons, including three as the NL leader in winning percentage. Twice a 20-game winner for the Cubs, he returned to the charmed circle with the 1915 Newark Feds before posting the last of his 185 career victories with the Braves a year later. One.

**6.** Constant flinging for second division teams kept this lefty from ever gaining the rep his talents deserved. Frequently a loser in high double figures despite some fine ERAs and a lot of shutouts, he had his best hour at 35 with the 1952 Reds when he won 17, had a 2.81 ERA and was an NL shutout leader. Eight years earlier he made the NL All-Star squad despite losing 20 for the Phils. One.

**7.** The Reds' hill leader in the 1890s, he broke in with a flourish for the 1888 White Stockings when he won four of five starts and had a 1.07 ERA. Twice a 20-game winner, an overall victor 176 times in eleven seasons, his agile bat won many games for him. Four.

**8.** The Cleveland National League entry didn't have much going for it in the 1880s except this great moundsman who twice led the NL in wins despite pitching for poor teams. Through at 31 after spending the 1887 seasons with Pittsburgh, he had 262 career wins and a stellar 2.43 ERA, one of the best in his time. Two.

**9.** Appearing in his first game with the 1894 Reds and his last with the same club 17 years later, he won 20 in the interim four times for the Pirates and twice for the Red Sox. Neglected today, this switch-hitting southpaw won 195 games. His slugging bat helped. Two.

**10.** Never a serious candidate for the Hall of Fame despite a .300 average, and remembered today only for his base-stealing exploits, this old outfielder's greatest achievement is totally overlooked. A five-time homer leader, mostly with the Philadelphia Associations, he held the all-time home run record before Roger Connor broke it in 1895. Also a four-time leader in runs scored and triples, he retired his bat permanently after the 1893 season. Two.

**11.** Twenty-nine the year he played in his first big-time game, he went on to play in nearly 1000 more and average .291. One of the few backstoppers in this century to hit over .350, he narrowly missed the NL bat crown in 1912. He hit .290 in four Series for McGraw. One.

**12.** Remembered as the manager who told his infielders to let Lajoie bunt on them in the hope the Napper'd beat out Cobb for the 1910 bat title, he put in 20 seasons behind the bat. Zimmer's remembered as the Spiders' backstopper in the '90s, but our man caught almost as often for them when not playing the outfield and was a far superior sticker. Lifetime .263, he later played with the Cards, Pirates and Highlanders. Two.

**13.** The White Stockings had better hitters in the 1880s, but their second-sacker was one of the true club leaders. Later with Louisville, he came back to Chicago for his coda in the late '90s and finished with 1671 hits. Dubbed "Dandelion," he remained in Chi when his playing days were over. Died in 1932. Three.

**14.** The Dodgers had another fine outfielder besides Wheat in the late teens and early '20s. Our man's peak years were 1919 through 1923. The NL's RBI and slugging leader in 1919, he also led twice in triples. An early day Tommy Henrich type. Two.

**15.** His apex was 1936 when in his first regular season he rapped .345 for the A's. But he had many more .300 seasons and played till he was 40 before calling it quits in 1951 after returning to the A's from stopovers with the White Sox and Red Sox. In the 1946 Series he clubbed .417. Steady overall, he could be spectacular at times; he once stole 56 bases in a season and another time he pounded 25 homers and 208 hits. You'll find his name on the all-time hit list ahead of many who are in the Hall of Fame. One.

*Potential Hits: 15*
*Potential Points: 27*
*Bonus Points: 0*

*(Answers on Page 173)*

Game

7

# One-Year Wonders

*Far and away your toughest inning of the year. If you can score more than one hit here, they'll be looking to retire your number one day. You're a definite candidate for the baseball experts' Hall of Fame.*

**1.** They called him "Goat," and his single season as the .206 hitting right-fielder for the runner-up Pirates in 1907 might explain why. Still, he walked only three times less than Roy Thomas, the league leader, and swiped 27 sacks. Obviously the talent was there, but it was not enough for an encore. Two-run homer.

**2.** How about this other 1907 palooka who came over to the Braves from the Cubs early in the season and mishandled their left-field job to the tune of a .211 batting average and a .920 fielding average, the league's worst among regular gardeners? Three-run shot.

**3.** Baseball's most awful club ever, the 1899 Spiders, had a big rookie right-hander who managed to complete all 26 of his starts and tie Hughey for the staff lead in wins. That victory total, however, stood at only four, and as he had 22 losses to go with it, no one wanted his arm thereafter. Grandslam.

**4.** The war-sapped Reds gave this Cuban righty a mound job in 1944, and he came in with a 9-9 record in 191 innings before going back to Havana. Four.

**5.** Another grandslam for the right-hander who worked 410 innings for the KC Association outfit in 1889 and came away with a 19-27 record and a one-way ticket home.

**6.** A two-run shot against your expert's rep that you don't remember the Cub second-sacker in 1895 who swatted eight homers and 76 RBIs as a rook and was never seen again.

**7.** Here's our lone one-year wonder who was less than 100 percent pure, in that he had a single pinch-hit appearance two years before he got his shot at glory with the Cubs in 1924 when Ray Grimes proved physically unable to handle the first-base job. Our man turned in an uninspired .261

before surrendering the bag to Charlie Grimm the following spring. Three-run homer.

**8.** Baltimore brought up the rear in the Association's inaugural season in 1882. Their main arm, as can be expected, led the league in losses with 28. He had 12 wins to go with it, however, and a respectable 3.32 ERA. It's totally up for grabs why he never pitched in the bigs again. Grandslam.

**9.** One final Association mound wonder. The 1884 Pittsburgh club was one of the league's worst, but perhaps their brightest light was this chucker who went all nine innings each of the 51 times he took the rubber. His 16-35 record was to be expected considering the little support he had. His exit surprised, however, and you'll surprise too if you connect for a grandslam on him.

**10.** His name was Clarence, but they called him Dutch—and in 1929 the White Sox called him one of their outfield regulars when he hit .258 in 103 games before his sun once again sank to the minors. Two-run homer.

**11.** If you miss this one, chances are you've drawn the collar all the way through this inning. Three bases for the Dodger righty who was 7-7 in 22 games that were split about equally between the bullpen and starting roles in 1952. His final bigtop toss came in the 8th inning of the fourth Series game that fall when he served up the triple to Mantle that iced Reynolds' 2-0 shutout.

*Potential Hits: 11*
*Potential Points: 43*
*Bonus Points: 19*

*(Answers on Page 174)*

# 2ND INNING
# Wine for Water

**1.** Camilli's acquisition forced this Dodger to shift to left field in 1938 after he'd opened his career with two .300-plus seasons. A year later the Dodgers dealt him. One.

**2.** In 1961 Zoilo Versalles took the Twins' shortstop job away from his countryman who'd held the post in 1960 while the team was still based in Washington. Two.

**3.** This rookie's arrival made the Giants shift Lindstrom from third to the outfield in 1931, and Lindy was never quite the same player again. Three.

**4.** Kluzewski's maturation in 1948 signaled the end of regular duty for the NL journeyman who'd handled the Reds' gateway post in 1947. Three.

**5.** The emergence of Walker Cooper as a full-timer in 1942 allowed the Cards to ship off this longtime NL star backstopper. One.

**6.** Grandslam for the three-year Senator center gardener who relinquished his job to Clyde Milan in 1908.

**7.** When George Kell nailed down the A's third-base job in 1944, what 34-year-old hanger-on lost his post but saw his career take on a new dimension when he was dealt to another AL club and installed at a different infield position where he played regularly for the next five seasons? Two.

**8.** Del Ennis brought the curtain down on the big league career of one of the great baseball names of the '40s when he claimed the Phils' left-field job in 1946. Del's predecessor had the job in 1945, one of his few bigtop seasons as a regular, though for many years he was a star in the minors. You'll recognize the name, but three says you don't recall it on your own.

**9.** The Waners were playing side by side in the Pirate outfield by 1927. Lloyd was a frosh that year, but Paul had come up in 1926. For one, name the two Hall of Famers who lost their jobs in the Pirate garden to these sib stars. Must get both to score.

**10.** Another entombed name from the '40s, he lost the Browns' third-base job to Dillinger late in 1946 and the Senators' shortstop slot to Sam Dente after the 1948 season. Ten years earlier he'd been chased off third base for the Tigers by Pinky Higgins. Two.

**11.** After the 1902 season which saw him solidify his rep as one of the NL's top performers, he jumped to the AL, grabbed Ducky Holmes' job out from under him and held it for the next 14 years. Slim clues these, but enough for sharpies to bingle.

**12.** George Treadway wasn't a bad ballplayer. He rapped .328 for the 1894 Dodgers and smacked 26 triples. He'd come to the Dodgers before the 1894 season from another NL team, however, and the man who'd bumped him out of

Who batted .185 and made 98 errors in one season?
(Question 14)

the right-field job he'd held in 1893 stroked a cool .371 in his first year as a regular. For one, who was that future Hall of Famer?

**13.** In 1932, his first year as a full-timer, he knocked Clyde Sukeforth out of a job. Two.

**14.** Terry Turner, for years one of the AL's finest infielders, grabbed the Indians' shortstop job for keeps in 1904. A grandslam if you know the immortal he replaced who was coming off his second successive .185 season and had just finished posting an .869 fielding average and a near incredible 98 errors.

*Potential Hits: 14*
*Potential Points: 30*
*Bonus Points: 6*

*(Answers on Page 174)*

---

3RD INNING
# Hose

---

**1.** Your eyes should get as big as saucers when you see a homer go up on the board for the name of the Union Association's top arm in 1884. A 40-game winner, he never pitched another inning in the bigs after that season. Baltimore had him at the time, and the Philadelphia Associations had him in his only other big league outing two years earlier.

**2.** They called him "Kickapoo"; and though he won 24 games as a rook in 1908, he was a disaster in the Series that fall and again in 1909, losing all four of his starts and getting shelled hard. Last appeared in 1912. That Series record stands as the worst ever among hurlers in four or more decisions. Two for this Bengal.

**3.** One of the AL's top relievers in 1969 and again in 1970, he slipped badly when dealt to the Red Sox in 1971 and is already a rather dim memory less than four years after he appeared in his last game. In 45 efforts in 1969 he was 7-2 with a 1.36 ERA and 22 saves. An Angel rook at the time, he was a good sticker; and some thought he could make it with his bat when his arm sagged. One.

**4.** The oldest rookie ever to go on to a 20-year career, he also became the oldest ever to win an ERA crown for the first time when he led the AL in 1959 at 36. Plenty there to wire you up for one.

**5.** His final big league game was a losing start in the 1903 Series. Before then he'd won 20 four times for the Dodgers and was one of the best hitting hurlers every to play the game. Solid throughout his long career, he's still one of the Dodgers' all-time leading winners. Three.

**6.** After five years in double figures, this NL workhorse looked about done when he came in with a 7-13 record in 1954 and a 5.26 ER.ʌ. Six years later, however, he celebrated his 40th year by posting a 13-8 relief record with the defending AL champs. Clues enough for one.

**7.** In 1971 he became the last man ever, and one of only a very few hurlers in history, to win 20 games in under 225 innings when he went 21-5 in the AL. Finished in the NL in 1975. One.

**8.** He looked as if he'd make Dodger fans forget the after-taste left by Rex Barney when he won 14 in 1960 and fanned 175 in 207 innings. Five years later, however, he was floundering in the minors. And five years after that? Well, that'd be 1970 and all he did then was rack up a 10-1 mark for the Twins and knock off 15 saves. One.

**9.** At 29 this star hurler of the '90s had 207 wins, but he never scored another. A 35-game winner with the 1891 Browns, he won 35 more for the Braves a year later and was last in the charmed circle in 1896. When not on the mound, he frequently played the outfield, and his .297 lifetime average attests to his overall ability. Ignored today by the Old Timers' Committee, he's got far superior stats to many they've installed in the Cooperstown Club. Two.

**10.** Over the years between 1955 and 1961 he worked more innings than any other AL hurler, twice won 20, several times led the league in starts and complete games—and yet never won the Cy Young award. It wasn't as if he made hay against the weak sisters either, for his main rep came from knocking off the AL's best. That last clue makes this just one.

**11.** He won 16 games for the 1925 A's and 20 for the 1928 Browns. In 1929 and again in 1931 he was an AL leader in starts. Also in 1931 he led in losses. With all that and the added info that he worked nearly 2000 innings in the majors, I still feel absolutely safe in offering a two-run homer for him.

**12.** Another forgotten 20-game winner was this Redleg ace who was in the charmed circle three times in the '20s, the last in 1926 when he was one of the NL leaders in wins. Like our previous man, he also led twice in starts and worked in the vicinity of 2000 innings—2112.1 to be exact. For him, though, I don't quite feel secure enough to offer more than three.

**13.** At 30 he had only 29 wins, but he went on to win 172 before he quit in 1959. In two Series in the '40s, he had the misfortune to pitch for some of the most dismal NL clubs ever assembled in the '50s but still won in double figures 11 years in a row and once won 20 for a team that won only 64. One.

**14.** This lefty's failure to win a single game in 1908 after winning 22 two years earlier was one of the key factors his club cited in explaining why the AL pennant flew elsewhere that season. His wing recovered a few years later, however, and he got on a pennant winner after all when he hooked on with the Miracle Braves as a spot starter. A semi-tough homer.

*Potential Hits: 14*
*Potential Points: 29*
*Bonus Points: 1*

*(Answers on Page 174)*

4TH INNING
# Nobody Knows My Name
# (1960-1977)

**1.** Nearly all singles this time, and most of them come a lot tougher than me. Put in the expansion pool by the Cards after coming to them from the Dodgers, I got claimed by the Astros for their inaugural season, and for four years I was their man at short. I once hit as low as .198, but the following year I jumped that by 70 points. For power, though, you could forget me. Except for catchers like

Tresh and Bergen, I was the all-time worst slugger ever among players in over 800 games. My slugging average was only 41 points better than my .236 batting average. The odd thing was, in a 20-game test with the 1958 Dodgers, I banged .391 and slugged in at .507. What a mirage! One.

**2.** Me and Bruno Betzel have something in common. I won't tell you what it is; you'll have to look it up. I *will* tell you I played a dirty third for both the Giants and Angels as late as 1973 and was one of the very few moderns who played a.k.a. for a time. Big year was 1971 when I hit .277 in 136 games in Candlestick. Flakey single.

**3.** With me it was either in the seats or in the catcher's mitt when I'd had my cut. Wham, bam, thank you, Sam—27 circuits in 1963 and 28 more a year later. The Nats interleagued me to the Phils in 1967, and those NL hurlers pretty well cut off my water over my last three seasons. One of those guys who had more career strikeouts than base hits, I don't want you to forget my arm. I had a bazooka out there in center, baby. One.

**4.** I'll bring two only because everybody seems to have forgotten that I got some Rookie-of-the-Year attention after my 1962 debut behind the dish for the Nats. I hit .285 in 109 games, and in a 16-game look the year before I did a .340 number. But my soph season I started losing my stroke, and by the middle of 1964 I was gone. The Nats had a lot of catchers in those years who were good for just a year or so, but none had my kind of promise as a rook.

**5.** I'm a snap single. Three times in the early '60s I was a .300 swinger, and in 1962 I led the AL in doubles. I won't tell you my main team, but I will say that Al dug me a lot—and he was a pretty good judge of talent, you know. Went to the Reds in 1967 but was about played out by then, though I did get in a fair amount of action with the A's and Red Sox in 1968. Record: .283 in over 1000 games.

**6.** They never thought I'd put it together; the Indians and Senators, that is. But when I got to the Royals in 1972 I went .300 in 134 games and did a .307 caper while splitting the following season between the Reds and Angels. A switch-hitter, I DH'd a lot when I wasn't playing the pasture. Speed wasn't my strong point—would you believe zero stolen bases in 462 games? One.

**7.** A fixture in the outfield for the Astros in the early '60s, in 1964 I came back to the Cards who'd swapped me to Roy's boys and tied an all-time Series record that fall when I rapped three pinch-bingles. The Cubs saw me last in 1965. One of those strange packages who batted right and threw left. One.

**8.** A guy with a world of stuff who never quite found a way to corral it is how they thought I'd be remembered. But after a two-year sojourn in the minors I made it back big in 1977. Got off the ground with the 1970 Reds and went over to the Indians for 1972 in the Uhlaender deal. Won 15 for the Tribe over the next two seasons and saw a lot of action in the lakefront bullpen in 1974 before hitching on with the Cubs for a brief look in 1975. One.

**9.** Remember me—the righty who won 19 for the 1964 Tigers after being the A's top chucker the year before? I tailed off after that, but as late as 1969 I was still around—with the A's again—coming out of their bullpen with my tall arm. One.

**10.** If you got that Tiger, you'll zap me for a bingle too. I won three more games lifetime than he did, after all, and even though I never had that one big year, I was one of the Phils' hardest workers in the early '60s before being swapped to the Pale Hose in 1962. In Chitown I twice won in double figures and threw some 13 shutouts over the next five seasons, including four in 1966 when I only won six games. The Astros got some neat bullpen work out of me in my 1968 finale.

**11.** Now, I'll be rugged. Although I toiled in over 200 games for the Indians in the '60s, you're in for a test. My left arm was strictly tailored for the bullpen, and even there it was so shaky at times that the Indians gave me a two-year vacation from the bigs after 1963 before calling me back in 1966 for my final two seasons of work. Best as a rook in 1961; 3-2 in 48 games. But my last fling wasn't bad—a 2.98 ERA in 47 games and five saves for the Tribe. Three.

**12.** Getting a little pitcher-weary? Don't fall out yet; you've still got me. Through the '60s I tossed 'em in for the White Sox, A's, Yankees, Pilots and then the A's again after they moved to Oakland. Some decent years ... ten wins for KC in 1965 and 11 more the following year, which I split between the A's and the Yankees. I slipped some after that, though I did have good days now and then with those Pilots. Two in your column for bringing my name to mind for the first time in already too many years.

**13.** Your turn, Senator fans, to score a grandslam. Well you should, because I played a lot of first in DC in '63 and '64 and was your main pinch-stick. I was already past 30 by then, but the Nats were kind enough to bring me back for a spell in 1966. Rig's boys were my first outfit in 1962, but the Nats were my real gang. Gil liked my glove so well he put it at both second and third on occasion.

**14.** I'm waving to you now, with that same big wave I used to treat Senator and Twin fans to after parking one. Pounded 11 seat-rattlers for the Nats in 1969 and 16 more for the Twins a year later in only 258 at-bats. My downfall was that I came along before the DH rule because I was weak in the pasture—no argument. But right from the start—in 1965 when the Nats gave me a short peek at AL arms—I began riding them out. Ride me now for two and then wave back.

*Potential Hits: 14*
*Potential Points: 22*
*Bonus Points: 3*

*(Answers on Page 174)*

---

# 5TH INNING
# Team Teasers

**1.** In 1943 an NL club gave jobs to two rookie southpaws who were born just five days and a few miles apart 29 years earlier in Oklahoma. The lefty from Loyal came through with an 8-2 record mostly as a starter, and the Broken Bow boy emerged with a 9-6 mark mostly in relief. For the remainder of their careers, however, they reversed roles. The Loyal lad twice led the NL in saves in the early '50s, while our man from Broken Bow won 20 in 1948, the year he also led the NL in shutouts, winning percentage and fans. Figuring out the team that got the two boys into the Series at times will help you get both of them for a bingle.

**2.** In 1937 this club was second in team batting with a .285

average. All three of their gardeners hit .325 or better, their third-sacker was one of the league's top sluggers, and they had two men among the top seven in RBIs. Yet this outfit lost 108 games, thanks to one of the worst hill staffs ever assembled; their moundsmen had an even 6.00 ERA and gave up nearly 200 more runs than the next worst staff. For one, name the club that proved once more and finally the importance of pitching.

**3.** Only twice in this century has it happened that neither pennant winner had a .300-hitting regular. Knowing that the two seasons came nearly 70 years apart should tune you in to both the years and the teams involved for a two-bagger. An extra deuce for naming the top hitting regulars on pennant winners in each of those seasons.

**4.** In 1921 the five top hurlers in the NL in mound appearances were all members of the same club. Each toed the rubber at least 44 times, each won at least 13 games and each worked over 234 innings. Never has a club had a pitching corps of such even depth. Yet this team, for all its super hill work, finished a distant fourth. For a single, name the team; extra point for each of the moundsmen you can name. Grandslam for all five.

**5.** This club set a modern record for having the pitching shorts when none of its moundsmen proved strong enough in 1957 to work more than 145 innings. It's the only time in history a team failed to have at least one chucker who worked enough innings to qualify for the ERA crown. Take one for naming the team and two more for nailing its mound ace who went 6-13 in 145 innings.

**6.** No club has ever won a pennant without having at least one flinger who worked at least 200 innings. The club that came the closest was the 1960 Yankees. One for naming their leading mound worker who clicked for 15-9 in an even 200 innings.

**7.** It's actually quite rare that a team doesn't have at minimum one chucker who goes over the 200-inning mark. There was once a club, however, that went three years in a row without having a 200-inning toiler. Oddly, this outfit was a solid contender throughout, twice finishing second. Telling you the years would make it too easy for you to name the club, so I'll just mention that their leading hurlers in those years were a former AL 30-game winner and the son of the last previous AL 30-game winner. The team's worth one and the exact years two more.

**8.** Only one post—World War II team has had three staff men over 40 years of age. Their manager would have been a fourth if he hadn't chosen to retire before the season. All three of these men worked more than 50 innings, all won at least one game and one is in the Hall of Fame. The manager clue should give you the club and the year for one. The names of the three elder moundsmen will bring three more; a single for any two of them.

**9.** The 1884 Mets were the first team to have two 30-game winners. For a double, what was the last team to have that distinction? Take two more for the correct year and the names of the two hurlers.

**10.** Those same two 30-game winners once worked 800 innings between them in an earlier season. Another twosome, however, set the modern record a year later by working 845 innings between them for a different club. For four, name the club, the year and the two chuckers. All are needed to score.

**11.** The 1890 Pirates were the last team to field under .900. The Browns were the last outfit to field under .950. For three, tell me when it happened, within one year either way.

**12.** In the early days most clubs got along on one strong-armed hurler who'd work four days out of five. The first club to successfully divide its mound duties between two men won the NL pennant and both its arms won over 20. Three for naming the two hurlers and the club—the first club, incidentally, to have two 20-game winners.

**13.** Watch out for this off-speed toss. Every regular on the Miracle Braves save one fell off dramatically at the plate in 1915. For a deuce, who was the only miracle worker who actually improved his batting average in 1915, albeit by only four points?

**14.** You've already been grilled about the Tigers who for years had two backstoppers who registered only two lifetime homers between them. During the war this AL team had a double-play combo who played nearly 800 games between them in bigtop competition and never hit a single homer. They played side by side all of 1944 and 1945; the second-base half was the shortstop in 1943 before his counterpart appeared on the scene; that counterpart had a slugging average only 26 points higher than his batting average (the smallest differential ever among players in over 250 games); and both were right-handed all the way and pretty fair base thieves. All those clues still add up to four if you know both the club and the impotent twosome. No credit for just the team, but knowing only one of the flea-flickers will bring two.

**15.** This last one's guaranteed to win you a round of free drinks at your favorite watering spot. Has there ever been a club in this century that finished second despite winning more games than the flag bearer? If so, what team was it? And when did it happen? Your clue, as if you needed it, is that it once did. Yep, look it up, and then shed a tear or two for the homer you missed for not knowing yet another odd and little-noted chapter in big league history.

*Potential Hits: 15*
*Potential Points: 46*
*Bonus Points: 3*

*(Answers on Page 174)*

---

6TH INNING
# Teen Terrors

**1.** For years he looked like the heir apparent to Ted Williams' job, but he wound up a 12-season career in 1964 without ever putting in a full campaign as a regular for any of his four AL teams. Age 19 when he first stepped to the plate in Fenway in 1952, his top showing was a .278 in 92 games for the 1959 Red Sox. Hit .240 lifetime and only 37 homers despite his rangy lefty-swinging frame that looked built for a big league suit. One.

**2.** At 19 he got his first look at enemy bats for the 1947 Dodgers. In 1950 he was 13-8 for the club that fell to the Phils in the season's last game. Only 22 then, he struggled on till the end of the 1956 season before the Orioles informed him that his 4-11 act wouldn't be invited back.

Loads of talent, but—like so many other Dodger arms in that era—he never quite found a way to use it. Two.

**3.** This Hoosier flamethrower was winning 13 for the Indianapolis NL club in 1888 when he was 18, and at 27 he had 243 NL victories. Bitter salary wars kept him from ever winning another game, and it took 80 years before the Old Timers' Committee woke up long enough to vote him into the Hall of Fame. One.

**4.** The Reds had him in their regular rotation in 1914 when he was only 19, and the following year he led the NL in losses. A 20-game winner in 1917, he was victorious for the last time a year later. All this happened before he was 24, and my guess is you'll have to live to be a hundred before you score three here.

**5.** One of the game's top coaches in later life, he's not generally remembered for his own big league exploits which began and ended pretty much before he was 20. With 10-12 for the 1918 White Sox, he got banged around a year later and departed when his wing and ego started hurting. The Senator lefty (of a few years ago) with the same last name was *not,* as some careless fans believed, his son. Three.

**6.** At 18 he was 18-41 for a dismal Indianapolis Association team in 1884; 20-13 for the Cinci beer league outfit a year later, he started off slow in 1886 and was bounced. Another of those kid wonders whose wings were clipped before he could vote, he'll get you a grandslam.

**7.** This next Association boy terror is only worth a two-run shot. In 1882 at 18 he registered the first of his three successive 20-plus win seasons for the Brownies. The Association's shutout leader in 1883, he was still effective after moving to Baltimore in 1886 but was dropped when he got shelled a few times upon returning to the Browns in 1887.

**8.** They both came up at 18, the elder with the Tigers in 1953 and his counterpart with the Cards in 1957. Teammates part of 1962 (the elder's last season), they were both primarily relievers; and the younger was so tough he lasted till 1974. By then he'd worked for 11 clubs in nearly 700 games. Why are they called counterparts? Because along with being teen terrors and travelers, they were name's-the-samers. Know one and you've got both for a bingle.

**9.** At 18 he started his first bigtop game, at 26 he looked about used up, at 29 he won the Cy Young award and at 33 he worked his last inning, with the 1971 Royals. Easy one.

**10.** The Cleveland Players League club had the pitching miseries and gave this 16-year-old lefty a regular job in 1890. A year later he won 20 in the Association, the last 18 with the Browns. At 19 he went 17-18 for the Cubs. At 22 he was told to pack up by the Phils. The youngest ever to win in double figures, he was also the youngest 20-game winner, but even knowing these two distinctions won't help you become the youngest ever to collect a three-run homer for him.

**11.** This NL righty went 14-8 as a 19-year-old frosh in 1967. He's had better years since but is still looking for his first 20-win campaign. One.

**12.** Nineteen when he won his first big league game in 1957 and 36 when he won his last for the 1974 Pirates, he had his top years with the White Sox, including a 19-9 in 1964. A power fastball was his chief asset, though in later years he blended guile with speed in a number of bullpens. One.

**13.** He hurled a shutout at 19 for the 1925 Yankees, but didn't win again until 1928. With the Bombers for parts of seven seasons, he won in double figures for them three times but never saw a moment of Series action. Later gave the Red Sox a couple of so-so seasons. Around till 1939 but only added three more shutouts to that teen whitewash job. Three.

**14.** Performing in a utility role for the Dodgers at 18 in 1944, he had to wait seven years before he won a crack at a regular job and then it was with the Cubs. Steady for them at second a couple of seasons, he later played center and third for the Reds. All he could manage was .220 as an 18-year-old, and he never really improved much on that, finishing at .236 for 14 seasons. One.

*Potential Hits: 14*
*Potential Points: 30*
*Bonus Points: 6*

*(Answers on Page 175)*

# Rookies

**1.** Easy toss goes back through my legs for one when you name the Card lefty who won 20 in his first full season in 1952. He never won 20 again, but he pitched some classic games, including one all of us would've given plenty to have been there to see.

**2.** We're stepping back in time to the frosh who went 14-37 in his inaugural for the Washington Associations in 1891. That start didn't discourage him from winning 20 twice for the Phils in the '90s or from making his last game—with the 1901 Dodgers—a triumphant one. Four.

**3.** With 14-5 as a Yank yearling in 1947, he won two Series games that fall, then tailed off sharply in 1948. Back for a reprieve with the Nats in 1951, he was good enough to win in double figures for them two years in a row and prove he wasn't just a frosh flash. One.

**4.** He went 18-9 for the Red Sox in 1912 and got into four Series games that fall, winning one. Went 16-14 a year later, then dropped to 9-12 in 1914 and grew disenchanted enough with the BoSox that he hopped to the Buffalo Feds in 1915 where he won 15 and led the renegade league in saves. The majors didn't take him back, though, allowing him to step down at only 26. Two.

**5.** Four bases for the Brave outfielder who started off with a fine .291 in 1931 and followed up by stroking .303. He never played even semi-regularly again and was last seen with the Cards in 1934.

**6.** How about the Highlander righty who led the AL in losses as a maiden in 1908? He came back to win 15 in 1909 and later was a Brownie and Tiger workhorse for several seasons. Two-run homer.

**7.** You'll be sad indeed if you miss bingling on the tall Giant southy who won 20 as a rook in 1937. Around as late as 1944, he was in double figures five more times but never again came close to the charmed circle.

**8.** Can't let you go without testing you on the Red Sox righty who scored a 13-8 record in 1959. The Sox couldn't believe he would be yet another of their yearlings who'd be knocked out by the sophomore jinx; but, alas, he took one of the worst tumbles of all, for he won only four more times over the next three seasons. Two.

**9.** Few started better than this White Stocking righty who won 43 in 1880 and led the NL in fans. The following year he led the NL in wins and was its ERA champ in 1882; but by 1885 he'd pretty well shot his flipper, and six years later he was dead. Still, in his first five seasons he won 172 games. Think where he'd be if he'd had another five years like that. Two.

**10.** Nobody touted him for Rookie of the Year after he was 8-2 in 40 games for the 1948 Braves, but his bullpen work had a large hand in bringing the NL flag to Beantown. After a couple of less effective seasons with the Braves, he went on to give the Browns and Yankees some so-so relief work before exiting in 1952. Two.

**11.** He was 17-15 for the Bengals in 1901 and the other half of their rookie-wonderman combo, and he did his counterpart Miller one better when he led the AL in ERA in 1902. Moving on then to the Browns, he was dropped mysteriously by them after the 1904 season but returned in 1906 to give the Tigers two more solid seasons before slipping away in 1908. Three.

**12.** A tough homer even for Cinci fans goes out for the handle of the rook outfielder who rapped .327 as the Reds' first-line left-fielder in 1934. A handful of games that added up to .176 marked his exit after 1935.

**13.** At one time considered the fastest man ever to play the game, he broke in with 33 stolen sacks and an even .300 average as the Reds' left-field man in 1929. Oddly, even though his hitting and stealing continued to be excellent throughout his brief career, he had trouble holding a steady job and departed after a .298 season with the White Sox in 1934. Earning a .303 lifetime, his last year was the only one in which he slipped below the .300 mark. The fastest-man-out-of-the-blocks clue makes this only one.

**14.** The pride of Palm Beach High School where he managed the football teams on which Burt Reynolds starred, he was so small as a senior there they called him "Peanut." But he grew to big league stature by 1961 and hit .280 as the

A's shortstop while stealing 37 sacks. Injuries slowed him thereafter, though he did give the Indians several years of regular work. One.

*Potential Hits: 14*
*Potential Points: 32*
*Bonus Points: 1*

*(Answers on Page 175)*

---

# 8 TH INNING
# Not with a Whimper

**1.** Baseball couldn't hold this early day star past his 28th year; he left the game after a .325 finale with the 1899 Cubs, taking with him a .330 average over seven seasons and a rep as one of the NL's top flychasers. The Hall of Fame might well have beckoned to him if he'd stayed around a while longer. His nickname would give it away, so of course you'll have to single without it.

**2.** Another of the many chuckers who gave the Dodgers good service in the early 1900s (only to be disposed of later like scrap paper) was this erstwhile Cub and Brave righty who went 11-16 in 227 innings for a poor Dodger entry in 1906 before departing at only 27. Had 8-17 as a Cub rook in 1901. Two-run shot.

**3.** Through at 26 after an 11-10 season for the 1901 Orioles, he won 20 for the Orioles' NL entry four years earlier and was a big winner in the NL all through the late '90s before jumping to the AL midway through the 1900 season. Three.

**4.** The 1927 Yankees had two outstanding hurlers who never won another big league game. One we've met elsewhere; this one, a lefty, went 13-6 in his only full season in the Bronx. Scoring 19-6 with the Reds in 1919, he won 21 for the Dodgers three years later, his top effort. Also 18-7 with the 1925 Nats, his left arm seemed to spell "pennant" wherever it went. One.

**5.** You recall the star Pittsburgh Rebel third-sacker we asked you about a few games earlier in this same category?

Well, the Terrapins' hot-corner man was nearly as good. After several years as a Phil utility man, he jumped to the Feds in 1914 and registered marks of .308 and .294 in his only two seasons as a big league first-stringer. Another blackballed Fed ace was the man his managers called "Runt." Homer.

**6.** The fickle Dodgers shipped this righty to the Highlanders late in the 1904 campaign because he was only 5-15. What they failed to note was his 1.68 ERA at the time which narrowly missed being the league's best. Another victim of the general Dodger silliness in those years, this Texan jumped to Milwaukee from the Cubs after the 1900 season and spent most of 1902 with the White Sox before going to the Bums. He died at only 34 in 1908, just four years after his final outing with the Highlanders. Two-run homer.

**7.** After several years with the Red Sox, this lefty looked as if he was done when he came to the Browns in his 34th year in 1941. But he didn't bow out till he'd gone 8-11 for the 1948 Pirates and flipped two shutouts. Also with the Dodgers for a while, his 13-8 season in 1944 was his best—though he won 13 again for the Pirates in 1946. Age only seemed to ripen his crafty left wing. Two.

**8.** Would you believe still another Dodger hurler in the early 1900s who got handed the short straw after a fine season? Try the righty who went 12-14 in 1907 with a 2.27 ERA. In his three years with the Bums he numbered ten shutouts among his 35 wins. No question that if all the Dodger mound rejects in those years had been put on the same staff and allowed to hurl their own way, the Bums would have been contenders instead of NL tail-draggers. Three.

**9.** This Redleg retread found a haven with the lowly Pirates in 1953 and 1954. Coming out of their bullpen over 50 times each season, he was their main stopper. In his 1954 finale he registered nine saves in 58 outings and was their only hurler to post a .500 record. Three.

**10.** The NL's workhorse for the Giants in 1899 and again in 1900, he jumped to the AL Nats after leading the NL with 22 losses. A Nat bulwark for the next two seasons, he left after an 11-17 effort in 1902. "Doughnut Bill" took his share of pastings, true, but he was about as long on stamina as they came in those years. Four.

**11.** He got to the Tigers just in time to appear in the 1945 Series. Went 13-19 in the 1945 season, most of it with the Braves. He'd been an NL mainstay for nearly a decade by then and was one of the top slugging hurlers in the game. Numbered five homers among his 14 hits in 1945. Forties fans will agree this is only worth one.

**12.** Still good enough at 35 to hit .310 for the 1927 Red Sox in 111 games, he'd led the Feds in hits as far back as 1915 and was for years after that the man who played in the same pasture with Ken and Baby Doll. A fine hitter in his own right, he went .341 in 1920 and .352 a year later. Close to 2000 hits. One.

**13.** After tying for the NL lead in saves in 1940, he won the crown outright in 1941. It was the era of Casey, Beggs and Mace Brown, but this Giant righty (and I do mean giant) was every bit as tough in the final act of his long career that saw him on the boards with the Cubs, Yanks, Indians and Reds before coming to New York. Two.

**14.** He and Hecker formed a one-two punch for the Louisville Associations in the 1880s. He twice won over 35 games, but his swan song for the 1890 Browns was nearly as fine. All he did was win 24 and fan 257 before departing at only 26. Homer for the lefty the beer league fans called "Toad."

*Potential Hits: 14*
*Potential Points: 37*
*Bonus Points: 2*

*(Answers on Page 175)*

---

# 9TH INNING
# Fall Classic

**1.** Start out as a winner by garnering a single for the only man to get ten hits in a Series that went the four-game minimum.

**2.** The Reds didn't have much to be pleased about in the

1961 Series. One who came through big, however, was their left-fielder who led the team in hitting. He played on part-time for a couple of years after that, but 1961 was his last real glimpse of the limelight. Once regarded as a coming super-slugger, he never fulfilled the promise of his second season as a regular when he banged 40 homers and a .309 average in 1955. Cinci fans got a charge out of seeing him have that fine Series. One.

**3.** For all-around excitement the 1975 Series was probably the greatest ever. How quickly can you single by telling me the losing pitcher in the final game?

**4.** Several right-handers have won more than this man's five games in Series competition, but he's the top righty winner to post a 1.000 winning percentage. One of the AL's last 30-game winners, he last hurled in the late teens for the Dodgers. One.

**5.** This old Giant righty got into three Series in the '20s. During the regular season he sometimes started, but the fall saw him only coming out of the bullpen. His Series record stands at 3-0, giving him the best mark in fall competition for a bullpenner. Two.

**6.** It's pretty well known that Gomez's 6-0 Series record stands as the best among lefties, but for a bingle what other Yankee southy went 5-0 in the fall? Take the hint that his first Series was in another AL uniform, but all his decisions came in Bomber garb.

**7.** This lefty emerged as the star of the only Series in which he played. His mound act that fall is well known, but omitted from most baseball minds is the fact that his only big league homer came in that same Series. For one, who was this 215-game winner who won his first in 1963?

**8.** The last team to go through an entire Series without using a relief pitcher will get you two.

**9.** Among chuckers who appeared in more than one Series, the best three ERAs all belong to southpaws. The first two on the list, Brecheen and Ruth, are well known for their Series heroics. The third man incredibly lost two of his three Series starts despite posting an astounding 0.89 ERA. His first Series loss, oddly enough, was to Ruth in the memorable 14-inning clash in 1916, and his second came when his club was shut out 1-0 by Walter Mails. Equally odd perhaps is the fact that our man later took

Mails' place as the top lefty on the AL team that beat him in his final Series outing. Two.

**10.** The first man to steal ten sacks in Series action is generally overlooked on the lists of great base thieves, but he was actually one of the NL's best and was twice a league leader. One.

**11.** His three-run homer was crucial in the fabled ten-run 7th inning in the fourth game of the 1929 Series. Equally crucial was his two-run shot that tied the fifth game in the 9th inning and set the stage for Miller to double home the run that ended the Series. Not known as a slugger, he had only 43 homers in a 12-year career and never hit another in Series competition. Two.

**12.** The Cards' hitting star in the 1926 Series was their shortstop who emerged at .417 after going only .256 over the regular season. It was his only season as a Card regular, and when the Cards won again in 1928 he was such a seldom-used member of the team by then that he didn't get a single Series at-bat. Later a regular with the Phils and Pirates, he had only three homers in over 4000 at-bats in the bigs and one of those of course came in that red-hot Series. Two.

**13.** Another Cardinal who saved his best work for the fall was this catcher who got into three Series in the '40s with the Birds and two earlier ones with the Cubs. In his five fall outings all he did was hit .462 and tie the Series record for most career pinch-hits. A longtime bigtop backstopper, he also had several seasons with the Giants. Two.

**14.** End as a pro by scoring two for the only hurler to post four decisions in a Series that went less than seven games. Your clues are that the second game of the Series was a tie and that he bested Rube Benton in the sixth game finale.

*Potential Hits: 14*
*Potential Points: 21*
*Bonus Points: 0*

*(Answers on Page 175)*

One of the great base stealers and twice NL leader.
(Question 10)

# GAME 1

## 1ST INNING
## Outstanding Offenders

**1.** Mattie Alou. **2.** Charlie Gehringer. **3.** Bill Bruton. **4.** Tommy Griffith. **5.** Elbie Fletcher. **6.** Bob Bescher. **7.** Johnnie Fredrick. **8.** Cy Seymour. **9.** Jeff Burroughs. **10.** Vic Davalillo. **11.** Cesar Gutierrez. **12.** Charlie Dorman. **13.** Jack Clements. **14.** Cap Anson.

## 2ND INNING
## Unlikely Heroes

**1.** Beals Becker. **2.** Wayne Causey. **3.** Bobbie Avila. **4.** Birdie Cree. **5.** Ron Blomberg. **6.** George Altman. **7.** Adam Comorsky. **8.** Clarence Gaston. **9.** Jim Donely. **10.** Dick Nen. **11.** Reggie Jackson. **12.** Glen Beckert. **13.** Allie Clark.

## 3RD INNING
## The Unrewarded

**1.** Jose Cardenal. **2.** Jack Fournier. **3.** Tommy Corcoran. **4.** Kid Elberfeld. **5.** Gene DeMontreville. **6.** Augie Galan. **7.** Larry Gardner. **8.** Baby Doll Jacobson. **9.** Ron Fairly. **10.** Frankie Hayes. **11.** John Anderson. **12.** Bob Ferguson. **13.** Ossie Bluege. **14.** Spud Davis. **15.** Tommy Leach.

## 4TH INNING
## Sartorial Splendor

**1.** Braves. **2.** Athletics. **3.** Braves. **4.** Indians. **5.** Indians. **6.** Cardinals. **7.** White Sox. **8.** St. Louis. **9.** Phillies. **10.** Reds. **11.** Athletics. **12.** Cardinals. **13.** Red Sox. **14.** St. Louis Feds.

## 5TH INNING
## One-Year Wonders

**1.** Gair Allie. **2.** Scotty Ingerton. **3.** Elliott Bigelow. **4.** Sparky Anderson. **5.** Al Boucher. **6.** Charlie Malay. **7.** Mike McCormick. **8.** Red Morgan. **9.** George Cobb. **10.** Bitsy Mott. **11.** Dutch Schliebner.

## 6TH INNING
## Ole Man River

**1.** Wes Schulmerich. **2.** Coco Laboy. **3.** Bill DeLancey.

**4.** Gene Desautels. **5.** Aaron Robinson. **6.** Ed Cartwright. **7.** Pug Bennett. **8.** Johnny Butler. **9.** Lefty O'Doul. **10.** Jim Rivera. **11.** Paul Richards. **12.** Jim Poole. **13.** Charlie Babb.

## 7TH INNING
### Rookies

**1.** Wally Berger. **2.** Del Ennis. **3.** Jim Greengrass. **4.** George Barclay. **5.** Grady Hatton. **6.** Gene Baker. **7.** Bob Hale. **8.** Dan Ford. **9.** Sam Bowens. **10.** Lefty Davis. **11.** Rich Coggins. **12.** Bill Brubaker. **13.** Bert Griffith. **14.** Red Barnes.

## 8TH INNING
### Nobody Knows My Name (1900-1909)

**1.** Bill Bradley. **2.** Kitty Bransfield. **3.** John Heidrick. **4.** Homer Smoot. **5.** Jiggs Donahue. **6.** Red Kleinow. **7.** Jimmy Sebring. **8.** Andy Coakley. **9.** Harry Howell. **10.** Casey Patten. **11.** Dave Fultz. **12.** Hunter Hill. **13.** Togie Pittinger. **14.** Spike Shannon.

## 9TH INNING
### Hose

**1.** Erv Brame. **2.** Alex Ferguson. **3.** Hersh Freeman. **4.** Spud Chandler. **5.** Jim Brewer. **6.** Eddie Fisher. **7.** Bob Gibson. **8.** Clark Griffith. **9.** Russ Ford. **10.** Pink Hawley. **11.** Frank Foreman. **12.** Ed Brandt. **13.** Fred Gladding. **14.** Mace Brown.

# GAME 2

## 1ST INNING
### Wine for Water

**1.** Ken Boyer. **2.** Ferris Fain. **3.** Chris Chambliss. **4.** Fred Merkle. **5.** Ray Schmandt. **6.** Jim Bottomley. **7.** Jake Jones. **8.** George Gore. **9.** Dick Groat. **10.** Bert Niehoff. **11.** Ollie O'Mara. **12.** Billy Hunter (Hope you didn't go for Willie Miranda). **13.** Frankie Hayes. **14.** Maury Wills.

## 2ND INNING
### Monickers

**1.** Frank Bodie. **2.** Bill Lange. **3.** Jack O'Connor. **4.** Lou Ritter. **5.** Frank House. **6.** Jimmy Slagle. **7.** George

Whitted. **8.** George Tebeau. **9.** Win Ballou. **10.** Elton Chamberlain. **11.** William Dell. **12.** Bob Boyd. **13.** Moe Solomon. **14.** Forrest Jacobs. **15.** Claude Ritchey.

### 3RD INNING
### Nobody Knows My Name (1910-1919)

**1.** Dick Hoblitzell. **2.** Armando Marsans. **3.** Les Nunamaker. **4.** Al Demaree. **5.** Claude Hendrix. **6.** Duffy Lewis. **7.** Jack Lapp. **8.** Burt Shotton. **9.** Ward Miller. **10.** Eddie Murphy. **11.** Bernie Boland. **12.** George Suggs. **13.** Red Smith. **14.** Hal Janvrin.

### 4TH INNING
### Jack of All Trades

**1.** Dalton Jones. **2.** Sparky Adams. **3.** Klondike Douglas. **4.** Jack Dunn. **5.** Barney Friberg. **6.** Frankie Gustine. **7.** Erwin Harvey. **8.** Frank Isbell. **9.** Hal Jeffcoat. **10.** John Morrill. **11.** Dots Miller.

### 5TH INNING
### Team Teasers

**1.** Johnny Bassler and Larry Woodall. **2.** Philadelphia. **3.** 1973 Braves; Aaron, Dave Johnson and Darrell Evans. **4.** The Tigers that year had Trucks, Troutt, Newhouser and Tommy Bridges. **5.** 1896 Reds. **6.** Cards and White Sox. **7.** 1973 Mets; no one else even close. **8.** Eddie Stevens, IB; Danny Murtaugh, 2B; Stan Rojek, SS; Frankie Gustine, 3B. **9.** The 1905-06 Braves; the hurlers were Irving Young, Viv Lindaman, Gus Dorner, Kaiser Wilhelm, Vic Willis, Chick Fraser and Big Jeff Pfeffer; only Young was luckless enough to lose 20 on both editions. **10.** Ready, set, go—Tresh, Aaron Robinson, Red Wilson, Ralph Weigel, Phil Masi, Bill Salkeld, Joe Tipton, Gus Niarhos, Bud Sheely, Don Wheeler, George Yankowski, Joe Erautt, Sam Hairston and Eddie Malone. **11.** Dizzy Dean, Ripper Collins and Tex Carleton. **12.** The 1918 Red Sox. **13.** Mike Kreevich. **14.** Don Mincher.

### 6TH INNING
### It's All Relative

**1.** The Alous. **2.** Ed and Chuck Brinkman. **3.** Josh and Fred Clarke. **4.** The Ganzels—Babe, Charlie and John.

5. Garbark. **6.** Rene and Marcel Lachemann. **7.** The Gleasons. **8.** The Pattersons. **9.** Oscar Ray Grimes, Jr. and Sr., and Uncle Roy. **10.** Hub and Gee Walker. **11.** Charlie, Hugh and Andy High. **12.** Bob and Irish Meusel.

### 7TH INNING
### Teen Terrors

**1.** Lew Krausse. **2.** Silver King. **3.** Cass Michaels. **4.** Jim Baumer. **5.** Nelson Mathews. **6.** Joe Quinn. **7.** Sibby Sisti. **8.** Bob Williams. **9.** Carl Scheib. **10.** Robin Yount. **11.** Billy Nash. **12.** Cesar Cedeno. **13.** Joe Coleman. **14.** Milt Scott.

### 8TH INNING
### Get Your Z's

**1.** Adrian Zabala. **2.** Chris Zachary. **3.** Paul Zahniser. **4.** George Zettlein. **5.** Sam Zoldak. **6.** Bill Zuber. **7.** Norm Zauchin. **8.** Al Zarilla. **9.** Rollie Zeider. **10.** Benny Zientara. **11.** Eddie Zimmerman. **12.** Frank Zupo. **13.** Bud Zipfel. **14.** Guy Zinn. **15.** Frankie Zak.

### 9TH INNING
### Not with a Whimper

**1.** Charlie Deal. **2.** Buzz Boyle. **3.** Rip Cannell. **4.** Andy Cohen. **5.** Harry Danning. **6.** Ernie Gilmore. **7.** Bones Ely. **8.** Luis Aparicio. **9.** Ike Davis. **10.** Pete Kilduff. **11.** Charlie Irwin. **12.** Gus Felix. **13.** Art Fletcher. **14.** Bill Fischer. **15.** Ray Lamanno.

## GAME 3

### 1ST INNING
### The Unrewarded

**1.** Arlie Latham. **2.** Denny Lyons. **3.** Fred Schulte. **4.** George Case. **5.** Mike Mitchell. **6.** Vic Power. **7.** Ron Santo. **8.** Danny Murphy. **9.** Jack Smith. **10.** Hank Severeid. **11.** Riggs Stephenson. **12.** Jocko Milligan. **13.** Frank McCormick.

### 2ND INNING
### Odds and Ends

**1.** Ken Boyer, 1957. **2.** Louis Bierbauer. **3.** Sammy

Esposito. **4.** Roger Bresnahan. **5.** Lena Blackburne.
**6.** Moose McCormick. **7.** Buster Mills. **8.** Lloyd Waner.
**9.** Dick Radatz. **10.** Herb Washington. **11.** Stan Yerkes.
**12.** Ruth, Smokey Joe Wood and Johnny Cooney.
**13.** Willie Kamm and Heinie Groh. **14.** Joe Kelley, King
Kelly, George Kelly and Pat's brother, Leroy.

3RD INNING
## Managerial Meanderings

**1.** Bobby Wallace. **2.** Jimmy Wilson. **3.** George Wright.
**4.** Jack Barry. **5.** Joe Quinn. **6.** Harry Wright. **7.** Billy
Barnie. **8.** Earl Weaver. **9.** Chick and Jake Stahl.
**10.** Frank Selee. **11.** John McCloskey. **12.** Jim Mutrie.
**13.** Pants Rowland. **14.** King Kelly.

4TH INNING
## Death in the Afternoon

**1.** Joe Cassidy. **2.** Hub Collins. **3.** Jim Doyle. **4.** Al Storke.
**5.** Hal Carlson. **6.** Walt Lerian. **7.** Mike Powers. **8.** Mike
Miley. **9.** Alex McKinnon. **10.** Jim Fogarty. **11.** Paul
Edmundson.

5TH INNING
## Who'd They Come Up With?

**1.** Giants. **2.** Dodgers. **3.** Pirates. **4.** Astros. **5.** Rangers.
**6.** Athletics. **7.** White Sox. **8.** Indians. **9.** Braves.
**10.** Cards. **11.** Indians. **12.** Yankees. **13.** Braves. **14.** Cards.
**15.** Indians.

6TH INNING
## Rookies

**1.** Marv Breeding. **2.** Vance Dinges. **3.** Les Fleming.
**4.** Ed Bouchee. **5.** Jimmy Hall. **6.** Johnny Gooch. **7.** Zeke
Bonura. **8.** Chet Ross. **9.** Jacky Brandt. **10.** Carl Lind.
**11.** Bug Holliday. **12.** Alex Metzler. **13.** Leo Norris.
**14.** Spider Jorgensen.

7TH INNING
## Nobody Knows My Name (1920-1929)

**1.** Les Bell. **2.** Charlie Jamison. **3.** Johnny Mokan. **4.** Ben
Paschal. **5.** Earl Smith. **6.** Ted Blankenship. **7.** Elam
Vangilder. **8.** Walt French. **9.** Bibb Falk. **10.** Bill Regan.
**11.** Aaron Ward. **12.** Earl McNeely. **13.** Jigger Statz.
**14.** Zach Taylor.

## 8TH INNING
### Don't Fence Me In

**1.** Fred Beck. **2.** Jake Stahl. **3.** Stan Lopata. **4.** Ted Williams. **5.** Hack Wilson. **6.** Lou Gehrig, 1931; Ted Kluszewski, 1955. **7.** Roger Maris. **8.** Harmon Killebrew. **9.** Gavvy Cravath. **10.** 1925 Cards; Hornsby and Bottomley. In pre-modern days the 1884 White Stockings had four 20-homer men. **11.** Dave Kingman. **12.** Oscar Walker. **13.** Buck Ewing. **14.** Fred Dunlap did it with the St. Louis Union Association club in 1884.

## 9TH INNING
### Fifties Follies

**1.** Bill Werle. **2.** Ernie Oravetz. **3.** Jack Daniels. **4.** Al Federoff. **5.** Johnny Merson and Clem Koshorek. **6.** Cal Abrams and Chuck Diering. **7.** Bill Glynn. **8.** Harry Anderson. **9.** Herb Plews. **10.** Jack Phillips. **11.** Paul Minner. **12.** Gail Harris. **13.** Putsy Caballero and Eddie Pelligrini. **14.** Danny Schell.

# GAME 4

## 1ST INNING
### Walking Wounded

**1.** Vic Wertz. **2.** Moose Solters. **3.** John Hiller. **4.** Mike Shannon. **5.** Boo Ferriss. **6.** Jackie Hayes. **7.** Buddy Daley. **8.** Louis Sockalexis. **9.** Hal Smith. **10.** Bill Sarni.

## 2ND INNING
### What Was His Real First Name?

**1.** Cramer. **2.** Barbra. **3.** Thompson. **4.** Forrest. **5.** Chalmer. **6.** John. **7.** Herbert. **8.** Nicholas. **9.** Charles. **10.** Arnold. **11.** Lawton. **12.** Colonel. **13.** Everett. **14.** Wilfred. **15.** Roscoe. **16.** Eldon. **17.** Henry. **18.** John. **19.** Harry. **20.** Lancelot; and Yank wasn't a nickname either—it was his middle name.

## 3RD INNING
### Outstanding Offenders

**1.** Don Hurst. **2.** Joe Jackson. **3.** Tommy Henrich. **4.** Ted Williams. **5.** Dave Rowan. **6.** Sam Mertes. **7.** Paul Revere Radford. **8.** Marv Rackley. **9.** Thurm Munson. **10.** Tip

O'Neill. **11.** Babe Phelps. **12.** Al Simmons and Chuck Klein. **13.** Willie Keeler. **14.** Hughie Jennings.

4TH INNING
## Not with a Whimper

**1.** Ed Lennox. **2.** Amby McConnell. **3.** Fred Lewis. **4.** Billy Lush. **5.** Benny McCoy. **6.** Blondie Purcell. **7.** Hal Lee. **8.** Martie McManus. **9.** Bill Lauder. **10.** Tony Lupien. **11.** Henry Larkin. **12.** Maurie Rath. **13.** Joe Marty.

5TH INNING
## Hose

**1.** Bob Grim, 1954. **2.** Steve Hamilton. **3.** Joe Hoerner. **4.** Rich Gossage. **5.** Bobby Burke. **6.** Mickey Harris. **7.** Harry Gumbert. **8.** Steve Barber. **9.** Jack Harper. **10.** Paul Derringer. **11.** Ace Adams and Andy Karl. **12.** Remy Kremer. **13.** Amos Rusie and Bill Rhines. **14.** Gene Packard.

6TH INNING
## Teen Terrors

**1.** Bert Blyleven. **2.** Harry Harper. **3.** Norm Miller. **4.** Johnny Lipon. **5.** Phil Cavaretta. **6.** Dan Costello. **7.** Hank Ruskowski. **8.** Samuel Tilden "Jimmy" Sheckard. **9.** Carmen Hill. **10.** Greg Goosen. **11.** J. W. Porter. **12.** Dave Clyde. **13.** Tommy Brown.

7TH INNING
## Travelin' Man

**1.** Shad Barry. **2.** Tom Brown. **3.** Alex Johnson. **4.** Hobie Landrith. **5.** Lyn Lary. **6.** Paul Lehner. **7.** Eddie Robinson. **8.** Tuck Stainback. **9.** Jack Warner. **10.** Vern Kennedy. **11.** Dick Littlefield. **12.** Bob Kuzava. **13.** Burleigh Grimes. **14.** George Browne.

8TH INNING
## Wine for Water

**1.** Bobby Lowe. **2.** Milt Stock. **3.** Hank Bauer; Mantle played right as a rook. **4.** Sid Gordon. **5.** Carl Furillo; bet you forgot that Skoonj played center his first two seasons. **6.** Joe Tinker. **7.** Chick Gandil. **8.** Denny Sullivan. **9.** Clyde Barnhart. **10.** George Kell. **11.** Frank O'Rourke. **12.** Paul Waner; Elliott came up as a right-fielder. **13.** George Harper. **14.** Hank Greenberg.

## 9TH INNING
### Nobody Knows My Name (1930-1939)

**1.** Dusty Cooke. **2.** Alex Kampouris. **3.** Bill Knickerbocker. **4.** Frankie Pytlak. **5.** Lou Chiozza. **6.** Earl Grace. **7.** Les Mallon. **8.** Ernie Orsatti. **9.** Al Todd. **10.** Rabbit Warstler. **11.** Dib Williams. **12.** Clay Bryant. **13.** Jim Weaver. **14.** Ray Hayworth.

# GAME 5

## 1ST INNING
### Hall of Fame Middlers

**1.** Cail. **2.** Perry. **3.** Harry. **4.** Michael. **5.** Stanley. **6.** Leroy. **7.** Joseph. **8.** Glee. **9.** Peter. **10.** Benjamin. **11.** Roosevelt. **12.** Clifford. **13.** True. **14.** Constantine. **15.** Merrill. **16.** Trowbridge. **17.** Batholomew. **18.** Robert.

## 2ND INNING
### Ole Man River

**1.** Bill Hassamaer. **2.** Roger Wolff. **3.** Joe Beggs. **4.** Luke Hamlin. **5.** Connie Marrero. **6.** Wilcy Moore. **7.** Bert Humphries. **8.** Curt Davis. **9.** Sandy Consuegra. **10.** Dixie Davis. **11.** Bud Stewart. **12.** Ted Abernathy. **13.** Rip Sewell. **14.** Bob Klinger.

## 3RD INNING
### Rookies

**1.** Jake Woods. **2.** Jim Nash. **3.** Ricky Clark. **4.** Dick Hughes. **5.** Irv Noren. **6.** Grover Alexander. **7.** Ken Burkhart. **8.** Bill Hoffer. **9.** Fred Beebe. **10.** Bill McCahan. **11.** Alex Kellner. **12.** Ed Scott. **13.** Wiley Piatt. **14.** Mike Nagy.

## 4TH INNING
### Unlikely Heroes

**1.** Dave May. **2.** Jim Hickman. **3.** Dave Johnson. **4.** Doc Miller. **5.** Eddie Morgan. **6.** Hank Steinbacker. **7.** Mike Rogodzinski. **8.** Bob Porterfield. **9.** Eddie Klieman. **10.** Sammy Ellis. **11.** Luis Arroyo. **12.** Ray Pepper. **13.** Buzz Capra. **14.** Chick Fullis.

### 5TH INNING
## Minor League Magicians

**1.** Lou Novikoff. **2.** Ox Eckhardt. **3.** Don Bollweg. **4.** Tom Burgess. **5.** Frank Carswell. **6.** Frank Saucier. **7.** Herb Conyers. **8.** Paul Strand. **9.** Bill Kennedy. **10.** Rance Pless. **11.** Max West. **12.** Rocky Nelson.

### 6TH INNING
## Nobody Knows My Name (1940-1949)

**1.** Johnny Barrett. **2.** Leon Culberson. **3.** Danny Litwhiler. **4.** Eddie Miller. **5.** Walt Judnich. **6.** Tom McBride. **7.** Mickey Rocco. **8.** Buddy Rosar. **9.** Stan Spence. **10.** Maurice Van Robays. **11.** Emil Verban. **12.** Hal Wagner. **13.** Clint Conatser. **14.** Roy Partee.

### 7TH INNING
## Death in the Afternoon

**1.** Ralph Sharman. **2.** Doc McJames. **3.** Bugs Raymond. **4.** Tom O'Brien. **5.** Mickey Finn. **6.** Mickey Fuentes. **7.** Urban Shocker. **8.** Brewery Jack Taylor. **9.** King Cole. **10.** Danny Frisella. **11.** Darby O'Brien.

### 8TH INNING
## One-Year Wonders

**1.** Moon Mullen. **2.** Ham Schulte. **3.** Charlie Hamburg. **4.** Monk and Vince Sherlock. **5.** Gomer Hodge. **6.** Ham Iburg. **7.** John Keefe. **8.** Hank Keupper. **9.** Joe Martina. **10.** Dutch McCall. **11.** Ben Conroy. **12.** Dory Dean.

### 9TH INNING
## Switch-Hitters

**1.** Pete Rose. **2.** Lu Blue. **3.** George Davis. **4.** Jim Lefebvre and Wes Parker. **5.** Dan McGann. **6.** Walter Holke. **7.** Ripper Collins. **8.** Jack Rothrock. **9.** Tommy Tucker. **10.** Walter Wilmot. **11.** Ken Singleton. **12.** Roger Metzger. **13.** Jim Russell. **14.** Tony Mullane.

# GAME 6

### 1ST INNING
## Nobody Knows My Name (1950-1959)

**1.** Owen Friend. **2.** Bill Wilson. **3.** Freddie Marsh. **4.** Bob

Boyd. **5.** Jim Delsing. **6.** Dick Gernert. **7.** Don Lenhart. **8.** Harry Simpson. **9.** Dave Hoskins. **10.** Al Corwin. **11.** Bubba Church. **12.** Tom Brewer. **13.** Preston Ward. **14.** Bob Usher.

2ND INNING
## It's All Relative

**1.** Parrott. **2.** Johnny and Elmer Riddle. **3.** Joe and Luke Sewell. **4.** Lou and Grover Lowdermilk. **5.** Virgil and Jesse Barnes. **6.** Smith. **7.** Jesse and Art Fowler. **8.** Joe and Heinie Peitz. **9.** Dick and Slick Coffman. **10.** Cobb, Kelly, Schalk and Marquard. **11.** Bill and Ray Narleski. **12.** Jack and Bud Lively. **13.** Snake and Hooks Wiltse. **14.** Russ and Jake Miller.

3RD INNING
## Outstanding Offenders

**1.** Babe Herman. **2.** Joe Jackson. **3.** Frankie Frisch. **4.** Hoot Evers. **5.** Ray Jansen. **6.** Manny Mota. **7.** Mel Ott, 2876 hits. **8.** Jimmy Stewart. **9.** Al Kaline. **10.** Rod Carew. **11.** Joe Medwick. **12.** George Sisler and Jack Fournier. **13.** Dan Brouthers. **14.** Pete Browning.

4TH INNING
## Odds and Ends

**1.** Don Leppert. **2.** Elmer Smith. **3.** Earl Smith. **4.** Hal and Del Rice. **5.** Jeff Pfeffer. **6.** Si and Syl Johnson. **7.** Hub Northen and Denny Sothern. **8.** Harry Heilmann. **9.** Byron Browne. **10.** Gene Green. **11.** Jay Johnstone and Bill Robinson. **12.** Howie Schultz. **13.** Hornsby. **14.** First Base: Mickey Vernon, Charlie Grimm and Joe Judge; Second Base: Nellie Fox and Bill Mazeroski; Shortstop: Luis Aparicio, Bill Dahlen and Tommy Corcoran; Third Base: Brooks Robinson, Eddie Mathews, Ron Santo and Eddie Yost. Conceded that Robinson, Aparicio and Mathews will probably make it one day, but don't lay any bets on the others.

5TH INNING
## The Ignoble and the Ignominious

**1.** Buddy Bradford. **2.** Tommy Reynolds. **3.** Bobby Wine. **4.** Frank O'Rourke. **5.** Brooks Robinson. **6.** Howie Moss.

7. Killer Killebrew. 8. Gene Paulette. 9. Charlie Jones.
10. Hal Elliott. 11. Jim Walkup. 12. George Ferguson.
13. Ben Cantwell. 14. Floyd Baker and Mike Tresh.

## 6TH INNING
### Hose

1. Mike Marshall. 2. Harry McIntire. 3. Joe McGinnity, 1903. 4. Scott Perry, 1918 Athletics. 5. Al Orth. 6. None other than Pappas. 7. Nope, not Milty this time—Jim Perry. 8. Dale Murray. 9. Babe Ruth. 10. Tom Zachary. 11. Johnny Sain. 12. Kaiser Wilhelm. 13. Harry Krause. 14. Sandy Koufax, Johnny Cronin, Ted Lewis, Eddie Cicotte and Pete Dowling; Dowling of course is the homer.

## 7TH INNING
### Monickers

1. Dain Clay. 2. Earl Browne. 3. Pearce Chiles (One of the real oddball turn-of-the-century characters). 4. Paul Blair. 5. Stan Rojek. 6. Edward St. Claire. 7. Samuel Smith. 8. John Glasscock. 9. Clarence Yaryan. 10. Hank Arft. 11. Thomas Sullivan. 12. Bill Voiselle. 13. Fredrick Walker (Not the Dix). 14. Albert Ferris. 15. Bill Doak.

## 8TH INNING
### Jack of All Trades

1. Adonis Terry. 2. Bob Stafford. 3. Monte Warde. 4. Howard Shanks. 5. Wid Conroy. 6. Joe Yeager. 7. Walter Thornton. 8. Bob Smith. 9. Ed Kirkpatrick. 10. Lee Magee (Born Leopold Hoernschmeyer). 11. Pete Runnels. 12. Rene Monteagudo. 13. Ron Brand. 14. Watty Lee.

## 9TH INNING
### The Unrewarded

1. Tony Taylor. 2. John Titus. 3. Bobbie Veach. 4. Guy Bush. 5. Ed Reulbach. 6. Ken Raffensberger. 7. Frank Dwyer. 8. Jim McCormick. 9. Jesse Tannehill. 10. Harry Stovey. 11. Chief Meyers. 12. Jack O'Connor. 13. Fred Pfeffer. 14. Hi Myers. 15. Wallie Moses.

# GAME 7

### 1ST INNING
**One-Year Wonders**

**1.** Goat Anderson. **2.** Newt Randall. **3.** Charlie Knepper.
**4.** Tommy de la Cruz. **5.** Parke Swartzel. **6.** Ace Stewart.
**7.** Harvey Cotter. **8.** Doc Landis. **9.** Florence Sullivan.
**10.** Dutch Hoffman. **11.** Johnny Rutherford.

### 2ND INNING
**Wine for Water**

**1.** Buddy Hassett. **2.** Jose Valdivielso. **3.** Johnny Vergez.
**4.** Babe Young. **5.** Gus Mancuso. **6.** Charlie Jones.
**7.** Eddie Mayo. **8.** Coaker Triplett. **9.** Max Carey and
Kiki Cuyler. **10.** Mark Christman. **11.** Sam Crawford.
**12.** Willie Keeler. **13.** Ernie Lombardi. **14.** John
Gochnaur.

### 3RD INNING
**Hose**

**1.** Bill Sweeney. **2.** Ed Summers. **3.** Ken Tatum. **4.** Hoyt
Wilhelm. **5.** Brickyard Kennedy. **6.** Gerry Staley. **7.** Dave
McNally. **8.** Stan Williams. **9.** Jack Stivetts. **10.** Frank
Lary. **11.** Sam Gray. **12.** Pete Donohue. **13.** Murry
Dickson. **14.** Otto Hess.

### 4TH INNING
**Nobody Knows My Name (1960-1977)**

**1.** Bob Lillis. **2.** Alan Gallagher. **3.** Don Lock. **4.** Ken
Retzer. **5.** Floyd Robinson. **6.** Richie Scheinblum. **7.** Carl
Warwick. **8.** Milt Wilcox. **9.** Dave Wickersham. **10.** John
Buzhardt. **11.** Bob Allen. **12.** Fred Talbot. **13.** Dick
Phillips. **14.** Brant Alyea.

### 5TH INNING
**Team Teasers**

**1.** Harry Brecheen and Al Brazle. **2.** Browns. **3.** 1904
(Chick Stahl, top hitter); 1973 (Reggie Jackson, top
hitter). **4.** Braves; Dana Fillingham, Joe Oeschger, Mule
Watson, Hugh McQuillan and Jack Scott. **5.** The A's;
Ned Garver. **6.** Art Ditmar. **7.** 1938-40 Red Sox led by
Lefty Grove and Jim Bagby, Jr. **8.** 1947 White Sox had

Earl Caldwell, Thornton Lee and Red Ruffing. **9.** 1904 Giants had Mathewson and McGinnity. **10.** 1904 Highlanders had Jack Chesbro and Jack Powell. **11.** 1915. **12.** 1880 White Stockings with Larry Corcoran and Freddie Goldsmith. **13.** Hank Gowdy. **14.** The A's; Irv Hall and Ed Busch. **15.** The 1915 St. Louis Feds won 87 games, one more than the pennant-winning Whales, but finished half a game out.

## 6TH INNING
### Teen Terrors

**1.** Gene Stephens. **2.** Erv Palica. **3.** Amos Rusie. **4.** Pete Schneider. **5.** Frank Shellenback. **6.** Larry McKeon. **7.** Jumbo McGinnis. **8.** Bob Miller. **9.** Mike McCormick. **10.** Willie McGill. **11.** Gary Nolan. **12.** Juan Pizzaro. **13.** Hank Johnson. **14.** Eddie Miksis.

## 7TH INNING
### Rookies

**1.** Harvey Haddix. **2.** Kid Carsey. **3.** Frank Shea. **4.** Hugh Bedient. **5.** Red Worthington. **6.** Joe Lake. **7.** Cliff Melton. **8.** Jerry Casale. **9.** Larry Corcoran. **10.** Bobby Hogue. **11.** Ed Siever. **12.** Harlan Pool. **13.** Evar Swanson. **14.** Dick Howser.

## 8TH INNING
### Not with a Whimper

**1.** Bill "Little Eva" Lange. **2.** Mal Eason. **3.** Jerry Nops. **4.** Dutch Ruether. **5.** Jimmy Walsh. **6.** Ned Garvin. **7.** Fritz Ostermueller. **8.** Elmer Stricklett. **9.** Johnny Hetki. **10.** Bill Carrick. **11.** Jim Tobin. **12.** Johnny Tobin. **13.** Jumbo Brown. **14.** Toad Ramsey.

## 9TH INNING
### Fall Classic

**1.** Babe Ruth, 1928. **2.** Wally Post. **3.** Jim Burton. **4.** Jack Coombs. **5.** Rosy Ryan. **6.** Herb Pennock. **7.** Mickey Lolich. **8.** 1928 Yankees. **9.** Sherry Smith. **10.** Frank Chance. **11.** Mule Haas. **12.** Tommy Thevenow. **13.** Ken O'Dea. **14.** Red Faber, 1917.

# PERFORMANCE TABLES

Once again you can gauge how well you did by comparing your performance against that of some of the game's greatest stars. In this year's World Series you went to bat 870 times, 46 more plate appearances in all than last season. Hence you needed more hits to average .300; 261, to be exact. And in order to register a .500 slugging percentage you had to total a minimum of 435 bases. A .300 batting average and a .500 slugging percentage—those are the marks you need to be considered a star in Baseball Memorabilia. Anything above those marks and you're walking with the superstars.

Before using the tables below, compute your bonus points. Each bonus point is worth two extra base hits and four extra total bases. Ideally, when you've got your final totals, you'll be up there with Ty and the Babe.

## Batting Average

319 hits = .367—Ty Cobb
310 hits = .356—Joe Jackson
300 hits = .346—Ed Delahanty
296 hits = .341—Bill Terry
290 hits = .333—Eddie Collins
283 hits = .325—Joe DiMaggio
276 hits = .317—Roberto Clemente
270 hits = .310—Luke Appling
266 hits = .306—Dixie Walker
261 hits = .300—Billy Goodman

## Slugging Average

600 total bases = .690—Babe Ruth
552 total bases = .634—Ted Williams
530 total bases = .609—Jimmy Foxx
502 total bases = .577—Rogers Hornsby
485 total bases = .557—Willie Mays
474 total bases = .545—Hack Wilson
464 total bases = .533—Mel Ott
452 total bases = .520—Harry Heilmann
443 total bases = .509—Eddie Mathews
435 total bases = .500—Roy Campanella